SECOND EDITION

# Understanding Financial Statements

## A STRATEGIC GUIDE FOR INDEPENDENT COLLEGE & UNIVERSITY BOARDS

*This book was made possible through the generosity of*

SECOND EDITION

# Understanding Financial Statements

## A STRATEGIC GUIDE FOR INDEPENDENT COLLEGE & UNIVERSITY BOARDS

*John A. Mattie, John H. McCarthy, & Robert M. Turner*

WITH SANDRA L. JOHNSON, EDITOR

*Understanding Financial Statements*

*A Strategic Guide for Independent College & University Boards*

*2nd edition*

Copyright ©2008 by AGB Press and the Association of Governing Boards of Universities and Colleges, 1133 20th St., N.W., Suite 300, Washington, D.C. 20036

Printed and bound in the United States of America

Library of Congress Cataloging-in-Publication Data

Mattie, John A.
Understanding financial statements : a strategic guide for independent colleges & university boards / John A. Mattie, John H. McCarthy, & Robert M. Turner with Sandra L. Johnson, editor.—2nd ed.
     p. cm.
Includes bibliographical references.
    ISBN 978-0-9754948-9-9

     1. Universities and colleges—United States—Accounting. 2. Financial statements—United States.
I. McCarthy, John H. II. Turner, Robert M. III. Johnson, Sandra L. IV. Title.

LB2342.M365 2008
378.1'06—dc22

    2008047632

This publication is intended to inform discussion, not to represent or imply endorsement by AGB Press or AGB and its members. For more information on AGB Press publications or to order additional copies of this book, call 800/356-6317 or visit the AGB Web site at *www.agb.org*.

Original cover art: Robert Peterson

# Contents

# Understanding Financial Statements

## A Strategic Guide for Independent College and University Boards

## Introduction

*We all remember Cuba Gooding Jr.'s immortal line from the movie Jerry Maguire, "Show me the money!" Well, that's what financial statements do. They show you the money. They show you where a company's money came from, where it went, and where it is now.*[1]

Financial statements tell a story about an institution's resources, and knowing how to read them is important for board members. Finances influence every aspect of a college or university's existence, so it is critical for higher education fiduciaries to understand how to use financial statements effectively. Beyond the campus borders, external users—investors, creditors, federal agencies, donors, and other stakeholders—expect complete, timely, and accurate financial statements and use them to evaluate and make decisions about an institution. This book aims to help trustees—those who are financial experts and those who are not—better understand and interpret information from college and university financial statements.

## Financial Reporting and Financial Statements

*Financial reporting* is a broad set of activities that includes preparing financial statements among a myriad of other requirements. The goal of financial reporting is to "[communicate] … information about an organization's resources and obligations."[2]

*Financial statements* account for an institution's assets, liabilities, and net assets. Each one focuses on a specific aspect of a college or university's financial condition. The statement of financial position, or balance sheet, presents financial data in a highly condensed format, essentially forming a snapshot of the institution's finances. The statement of activities, or income statement, classifies transactions as either operating or nonoperating, so readers can easily assess how the college or university used its resources. Finally, the statement of cash flows details how an institution used its cash for operations, investments, and financing.

Because each college or university has unique circumstances that affect its accounting practices, it is standard to provide *supplemental information* and *supplemental data* that shed light on the financial statements. Supplemental information includes explanatory text and summary tables. It provides context for readers, making it easier to assess an institution's financial health. For example, preparers of financial statements might include text that discusses an institution's economic resources and how they were used during the reporting year. The formal name for such text is *management discussion and analysis* (MD&A), and it provides readers with management's assessment of the institution's financial health.

Supplemental data can be charts about nonfinancial factors (such as student demographics), or they can be

---

[1]  U.S. Securities Exchange Commission, "Beginners' Guide to Financial Statements," *http://www.sec.gov/investor/pubs/begfinstmtguide.htm*.

[2]  FASB, *Objectives of Financial Reporting by Nonbusiness Organizations* (Concepts Statement No. 4, 1980), par. 11.

performance indicators that measure how effectively the institution used its resources.[3] Supplemental data are so informative that many users of college and university financial information rely on them to enhance their understanding.[4] For example, enrollment trends and projections significantly influence an institution's ability to generate revenues, and hence cash flows, to meet debt and other financial requirements.

As we have already stated, this book focuses on financial statements. However, trustees should be aware of supplemental information and data, because they provide important details and justification behind the information in the financial statements.

## Why Publish a New Edition of *Understanding Financial Statements?*

Since we first published *Understanding Financial Statements* in 1997, the financial reporting environment has changed, especially from the economic, legislative, and social perspectives. As a result, we revised the financial statements in this edition to reflect some of these changes.

Ten years ago, colleges and universities began to adopt a new financial reporting model for not-for-profit organizations, and few "real-life" financial statements that used the new model were available. Consequently, the first edition's statements for the hypothetical institution, SanJo University, were relatively simple and limited. In this new edition we have modified the financial statements to reflect the many changes in reporting standards as well as some of the best practices that have evolved in the field. We also have created a five-year history of financial data reflecting economic realities that institutions have encountered in recent years. This robust data set allows us to better demonstrate how trends influence the financial assessment process.

Here is a brief overview of the book:

+ Chapter 1 discusses many of the strategic issues and trends facing higher education.

+ Chapters 2 and 3 together provide an overview of the technical environment. Chapter 2 focuses on the concepts behind financial reporting, while Chapter 3 examines specific information requirements for the statements.

+ Chapters 4, 5, and 6 respectively discuss the statement of financial position or balance sheet, the statement of activities or income statement, and the statement of cash flows.

+ Chapter 7 describes how external users, especially ratings agencies, might analyze an institution's financial statements. It also explains ratio analysis, with a focus on operating, financial strength, and liquidity and cash-flow ratios.

+ Chapter 8 explains how internal users might analyze an institution's financial statements. The analysis focuses on questions trustees might ask about tuition, financial aid, endowment, costs, and debt at SanJo University, our hypothetical institution.

+ Chapter 9 focuses on the audit committee's responsibility in a college or university's financial reporting process.

## Revisiting Our Objectives

In the post-Enron environment, the public has demanded more responsibility and accountability from governing boards, including those of colleges and universities. Accountability is the new watchword, since stakeholders have become more information-savvy. Colleges and universities must answer to sometimes skeptical constituencies, which include the public, legislators, the media, and others. Financial statements, then, are important for communicating the institution's financial story.

Additionally, independent colleges and universities are required to file annually an information return, Form 990, with the IRS. The IRS and tax exempt institutions must make the Form 990 available to the public (except for information related to contributors).

---

[3] SFAC No. 4, par. 11.
[4] Turner, "Examination of External Financial Reporting," (PhD dissertation, Boston University, 1992): 132.

In 2008 the Form 990 was significantly overhauled following a period of input to the IRS from across the tax exempt sector. What resulted was a lengthy document which became effective for the 2008 tax year. The new Form 990 was promulgated to meet policy maker expectations for increased accountability and transparency across the tax exempt sector, including independent higher education institutions. The new form, which consists of some 15 separate schedules in addition to a core form, focuses on compensation processes for your chief executive, endowment management, conflict of interest, and other governance related issues.

The IRS encourages boards to share and review the Form 990 with all board members prior to its submission—in fact, the new form explicitly asks if all board members received a copy. The process of board review will evolve for each board over the next several years; however, transparency argues for all board members to have the opportunity to understand the key elements contained in the form.

As the stewards of the institution, trustees must ensure the financial statements, including information required to be disclosed in the Form 990, are reliable, understand the story they tell, and interpret it to the community. We believe *Understanding Financial Statements* will help trustees accomplish these goals.

# CHAPTER 1

# Strategic Issues Affecting Higher Education

Financial issues affect the feasibility and timing of every strategic decision of a college or university. In this chapter, we explore several issues and pose questions for board members to consider when reviewing an institution's finances and making strategic decisions. The issues we explore are:

| | |
|---|---|
| · Pricing | · Costs |
| · Student financial aid | · Policies |
| · Nontuition revenue sources | · Investment risks |

The list is by no means all-inclusive. Board members and administrators also must consider significant institution-specific issues. Having both a detailed and a global view of the business environment gives context to the financial information used in decision making.

In this chapter we use survey data, primarily from long-standing annual surveys, to explore each issue. Because data points change each year, we advise trustees to look at the trends rather than the specific results for any one year. Our focus here is solely on the strategic issues themselves. We return to them in later chapters to explore how they relate to financial statements.

Before exploring the issues, we first must discuss a new trend affecting all businesses—both for-profit and not-for-profit. In recent years "accountability" has emerged as the defining strategic issue, and how to achieve it has become the key question.

## Sarbanes-Oxley Act of 2002

In 2002 Congress passed the Sarbanes-Oxley Act (SOX; Public Law 107-204) in response to the highly publicized corporate failures of energy giant Enron and long-distance provider WorldCom. The goal was to restore public confidence in the financial markets. Perhaps the most pressing issues have been the increased demands for accountability and transparency in financial reporting. In the post-Enron environment, stakeholders are holding trustees accountable for nearly everything that occurs under their watch, especially changes in an institution's financial health. At the same time, stakeholders want greater transparency in the reporting process. Consequently, they expect boards of trustees to understand the financial information their institutions disseminate and to respond appropriately to its financial challenges. In this context, financial statements must be comprehensive and provide clear and concise information, so informed readers readily can assess an institution's financial condition.

Although SOX applies only to companies with publicly traded securities, many not-for-profit organizations have voluntarily adopted selected provisions of the law. For example, audit committees must now have at least one "financial expert,"[1] and its members

---

[1] Section 407 of SOX defines a financial expert as someone who has thorough education and experience:

- An understanding of generally accepted accounting principles (GAAP) and financial statements;
- An understanding of audit committee functions;
- Experience with preparing or auditing financial statements;
- Experience in the application of principles surrounding accounting for estimates, accruals, and reserves; and
- Experience with internal accounting controls.

must be "independent" (that is, they may not accept any consulting, advisory, or other fees from the institution). In addition, SOX defines audit committee responsibilities as:

+ Overseeing, on behalf of the entire board, the organization's accounting and financial reporting processes as well as regulatory and audit matters related to the financial statements[2] and

+ Appointing, compensating, and overseeing the external auditor as well as preapproving audit and nonaudit services.

Colleges and universities have responded to SOX by bringing their audit committees more in line with the law's mandates. Many have enhanced their audit committee charters, reaffirming—or strengthening—their oversight of regulatory compliance matters, internal controls, the financial reporting process, and the external auditor. Others have established a separate audit committee, tried to appoint at least one financial expert, and considered independence issues. Also, some colleges and universities have anticipated possible state (for example, California) or federal charity-reform legislation and have used SOX to prepare for it. In short, colleges and universities are taking to heart the general public's concerns with accountability and transparency in financial reporting.[3]

## Pricing

Chart 1.1 shows the steady rise in college tuition and fees over the last 30 years. In fact, the price of a college education has increased faster than inflation in both the private and public sectors. In the past decade, tuition and fees at independent four-year institutions have increased an average of 5.5 percent per year, or 2.8 percent per year after inflation; for public four-year institutions, the increase averaged 7 percent each year, or 4.2 percent after inflation.

Because tuition is the major revenue source for many institutions, developing a long-term pricing strategy is

---

[2]  We explore this responsibility in greater depth in Chapter 9.

[3]  California enacted the Nonprofit Integrity Act in 2004, requiring certain not-for-profit organizations in California to establish audit committees and to have annual independent audits. The act also requires the governing board or an authorized board committee to review and approve executive compensation.

**Chart 1.1** Tuition and Fees in Constant Dollars, for Academic Years 1976-77 to 2006-07

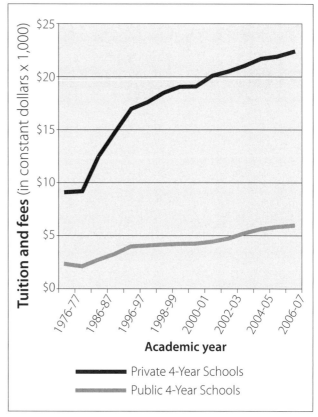

*Source:* The College Board, "Trends in College Pricing 2006," *http://www.collegeboard.com/trends.*

critical for the board. At what level will tuition—even after grant aid—become prohibitive at a specific institution? Clearly, pricing has major long-range implications for nearly all colleges and universities.

## Student Financial Aid

One of the most challenging issues facing independent colleges and universities—and one that is directly tied to pricing—is financial aid. Institutions try to meet shortfalls of federal and state financial aid with institutional resources in the form of loans and grants. Ideally, institutions award financial aid that is funded by investment income or designated donor support. When colleges and universities spend unrestricted funds for grant aid, they essentially lower the tuition charged to a particular student. Chart 1.2 shows how institutional grants have increased steadily over the last decade.

Institutional grants have risen because federally funded financial aid increasingly is composed of loans

**Chart 1.2** Institutional grants in 2005 dollars, 1995-96 to 2005-06

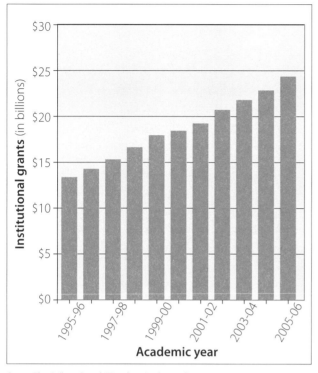

*Source:* The College Board, "Trends in Student Aid 2006," *http://www.collegeboard.com/trends.*

rather than grants. In fact, the largest component of student financial aid is federal loans, as shown in Chart 1.3. With much of their aid in the form of loans, students are graduating with increasing debt burdens.

## Nontuition Revenue Sources

Many colleges and universities rely heavily on a single revenue source: tuition. In fact, for some independent institutions it comprises 70 percent to 80 percent of their revenue. Furthermore, even if an institution has multiple revenue sources, individual schools or programs may rely on a single source. If anything affects that revenue source, trouble can quickly follow. Therefore, understanding an institution's revenue components, as well as its reliance on each one, allows board members to respond to changes and assess their impact on both operations and capital needs. Historical trends and future revenue projections under different scenarios can help board members respond appropriately if a shortfall in any revenue source occurs.

Besides tuition, important sources of revenue for colleges and universities are endowment income, research

grants and contracts, charitable contributions, auxiliary income, and, for public institutions, state appropriations. Next, we discuss trends in the first three revenue sources.

**Endowment income.** Generally speaking, colleges and universities with large endowments have more financial flexibility than those with small or no endowments. Endowment income provides a cushion in bad times, enabling institutions to fund operating or program deficits. However, endowment income varies significantly with the financial markets.

As shown in Chart 1.4, the average return fluctuated widely, from a 20 percent gain in 1997 to a minus 6 percent loss in 2002. While colleges and universities enjoyed double-digit returns from 1995 to 2000, they endured a period of low or negative returns before seeing double-digits again in 2004.

The fluctuating financial market is not the only issue affecting endowments. The gap between institutions with the largest endowments and those with smaller

**Chart 1.3** Student aid in 2005 dollars, 1995-96 to 2005-06

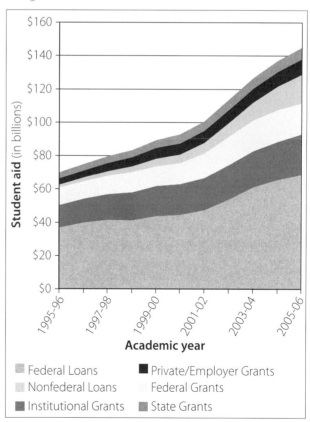

*Source:* The College Board, "Trends in Student Aid 2006," *http://www.collegeboard.com/trends.*

**Chart 1.4** Average endowment returns, 1995 to 2005

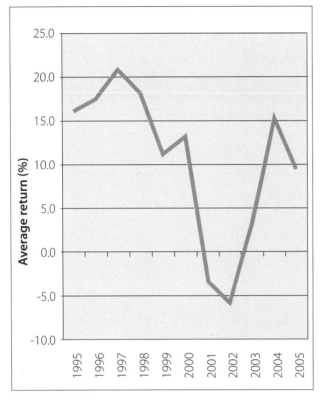

*Source:* Erin Strout, "College Endowments Post 'Respectable' Returns for 2005," *The Chronicle of Higher Education* (January 27, 2006): xx.

ones is widening in both overall size and annual performance. Institutions with endowments over $1 billion had average returns of almost 14 percent in 2005 compared to a return of just 7 percent for institutions with endowments of $25 million or less.[4] Colleges and universities with larger endowments can invest more heavily in instruments that carry a higher rate of return as well as risk, and they have the resources to hire top-notch managers who can handle more complex investments.

**Research grants and contracts.** Sponsored research funding is a significant source of funding for many universities, and the largest percentage comes from the federal government.[5] Funding for research comes from various sources, including state govern-

ments and institutional funds, and can vary from year to year. Chart 1.5 shows institutions have increasingly self-funded research since the mid-1980s.

**Charitable contributions.** Private donations are another important revenue source. Chart 1.6 shows private donations totaled $25.5 billion in 2005, representing a 4.9 percent increase over the prior year.[6] It also shows the volatility of giving: in recent years, the percentage change in annual giving has gone from minus 1 percent in 2002 to 4.9 percent in 2005.

Private donations are not increasing for all institutions. In general, the most wealthy institutions—those with the largest endowments—receive the most private donations. For example, in the 2005 survey year, 20 institutions raised more than $6 billion, accounting for more than a quarter of the total amount raised. Without exception, these institutions already had significant endowments.

**Chart 1.5** Sources of research funds, 1974 to 2004

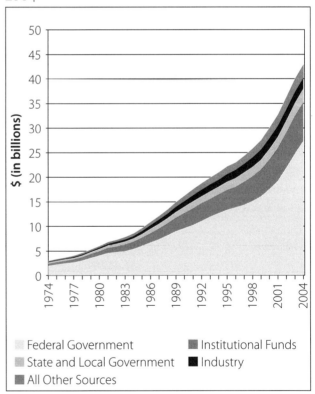

*Source:* National Science Foundation, "Academic Research and Development Expenditures: Fiscal Year 2004," table 1, *http://www.nsf.gov/statistics/nsf06323/.*

---

4   Also note that the blended return was nearly 10 percent in 2005 as shown in Chart 1.4. Strout, "College Endowments." *Note: The Chronicle*'s data is from the annual NACUBO Endowment Study, *http://www.nacubo.org.*

5   The second largest funding source is institutional funds; for the last several years, institutional funds have provided nearly 20 percent of total funding.

6   After adjusting for inflation, the percent increase in 2005 was 1.6 percent.

**Chart 1.6** Trends in giving to higher education, 1985 to 2005

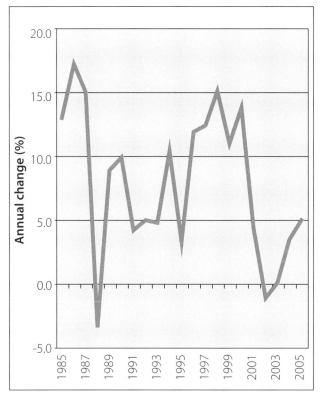

*Source:* Erin Strout, "In the Money," *The Chronicle of Higher Education* (February 24, 2006).

*Note: The Chronicle's* data are from an annual study by the Council for Aid to Education, *http://www.cae.org*.

## Costs

In addition to sources of revenues, board members must also understand an institution's cost structure. For 45 years, the Higher Education Price Index (HEPI), which is published by the Commonfund Institute, has documented the cost of goods and services typically purchased by colleges and universities. Chart 1.7 compares the annual changes in the HEPI and the Consumer Price Index (CPI) from 1975 to 2006. It shows the HEPI has been greater than the CPI for 23 years and lower than or equal to the CPI in only 9 years.

An understanding of the HEPI as a measure of overall costs is important for board members as they consider the growth in an institution's costs, even though nearly all institutions incur significant expenses for personnel and facilities.

**Salaries and benefits.** Higher education is a labor-intensive sector; consequently, salaries and benefits

account for a large portion of its costs. According to the College and University Professional Association for Human Resources (CUPA-HR), "human resource costs range from 65 [percent] to 85 percent of an institution's overall operating expenses."[7] In particular, colleges and universities have had difficulty absorbing the double-digit increases in the costs of employee health care benefits.

Slightly more than 80 percent of the institutions in the 2006 CUPA-HR survey reported an increase in the cost of medical and dental plans. The median increase in the total medical/dental plan cost was 9 percent, despite 11 percent of respondents reporting that health care benefits had been reduced. Table 1.8 shows how the median monthly costs for health care benefit plans increased from 2004 to 2006.

**Chart 1.7** HEPI versus CPI, 1975 to 2006

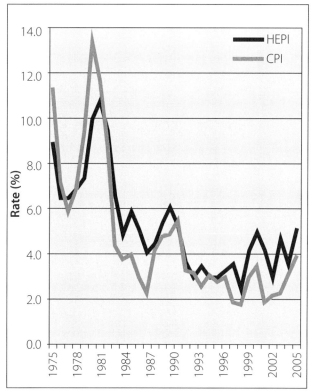

*Source:* Commonfund Institute, "HEPI 2006 Update," 3, table A, *http://www.commonfund.org*.

---

7   CUPA-HR, "Faculty Salary Survey," v.

**Table 1.8** Median monthly costs for health care plans by year

|  | **2004** | **2005** | **2006** |
|---|---|---|---|
| **Employee** | $59 | $71 | $84 |
| **Employer** | $282 | $311 | $326 |

*Source:* CUPA-HR, "2006 Benefits Survey Report," *http://www.cupahr.org.*

* The 2006 costs are for institutions that do not have consumer-driven health care plans. With consumer-driven health care plans, the median monthly cost is $75 for the employee and $314 for the employer.

Salary costs are not increasing as rapidly as health care benefit costs. According to CUPA-HR's annual survey, full professor salaries increased each year between 2004 and 2006, with independent colleges and universities reporting larger annual increases than public institutions.[8] Chart 1.9 shows the average salary increases for full professors at independent and public institutions.

**Chart 1.9** Faculty salary increases, 2003-04 to 2005-06

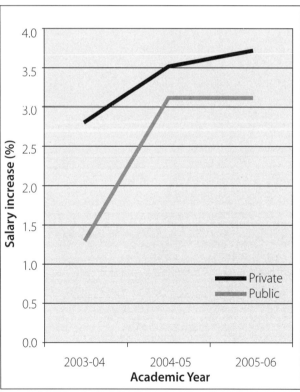

*Source:* CUPA-HR, "National Faculty Salary Survey by Discipline and Rank in Four-Year Colleges and Universities," 13, *http://www.cupahr.org/surveys/salarysurveysinfo.asp.*

**Chart 1.10** Administrative salary increases, 2003-04 to 2005-06

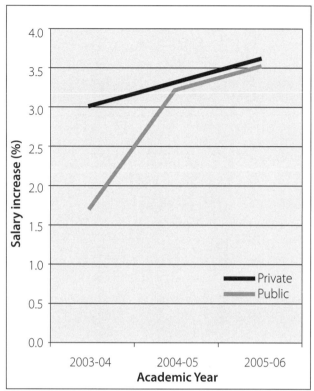

*Source:* CUPA-HR, "Administrative Compensation Survey," 11, *http://www.cupahr.org/surveys/salarysurveysinfo.asp.*

CUPA-HR also conducts an annual survey of administrative salaries. After performing a position-by-position analysis of institutions that participated in both the 2005 and 2006 surveys, it determined that the median salary increase for all types of administrative positions was 3.5 percent, as compared to a 3.4 percent increase in the CPI.[9] Chart 1.10 depicts the median salary increase across all types of administrative positions in independent and public institutions and shows the median salary increase at independent institutions was slightly larger.

**Facilities: Cost of maintenance and new construction.** Maintaining the physical plant is a major challenge for most colleges and universities. Today's students and families expect first-rate classrooms, laboratories, and housing; so the condition of an institution's buildings affects enrollment levels, the quality of education, and health and safety. Moreover, financial markets use capital maintenance needs to determine a college or university's long-term viability.

---

[8]   Ibid., xiii.

[9]   CUPA-HR, "Administrative Compensation Survey," 11.

Ensuring the annual upkeep of an institution's physical plant, which includes renovating existing facilities and building new ones, is a critical component of long-term financial planning. Colleges and universities must factor in additional costs for campus buildings that are historical treasures or those that were built for what was expected to be short-term use. When budgets are stretched too thin, colleges and universities may defer needed maintenance, but eventually, they must do the work.

How much maintenance has been deferred on a national basis? The Association of Higher Education Facilities Officers (APPA) conducts an annual survey to estimate the Facilities Condition Index (FCI), which is the deferred maintenance backlog divided by the current replacement value of campus buildings and their infrastructure. Chart 1.11 shows the FCI from 1999 to 2005 for public and independent institutions; the FCI of public institutions decreased slightly while that of independent institutions increased slightly.

**Chart 1.11** FCI for selected years

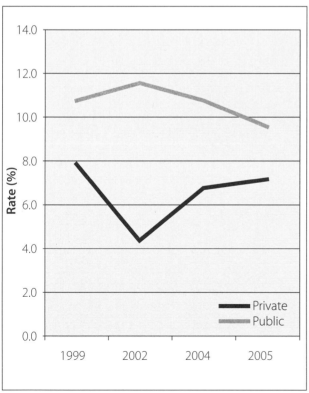

Source: 2004-05 Facilities Performance Indicators (Alexandria, Va.: APPA, 2006), 38.

**Chart 1.12** Amount spent for completed college construction, 1995 to 2005

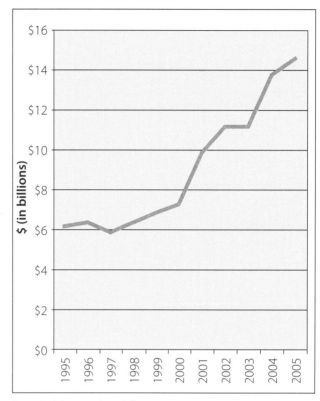

Source: Paul Abramson, "2006 College Construction Report," (Peter Li Education Group, February 2006), C3, table 1, http://www.peterli.com/cpm/resources/rptscpm.shtm.

In 2005, completed construction projects at colleges and universities totaled $14.5 billion,[10] which was the highest one-year total ever. Institutions spent nearly $10 billion on new buildings; $2 billion on additional space in existing buildings; and $2.5 billion on renovations. Chart 1.12 shows the $14.5 billion total for 2005 as well as the steady increase in the amount spent between 1995 and 2005.

The "Construction Report" also noted that construction projects for 2006 totaled approximately $28.4 billion—$14.4 billion on projects nearing completion and $14 billion on projects scheduled to begin. With the higher costs of borrowing and foreign markets, particularly China, using more construction commodities, costs are expected to increase.

---

[10] Abramson, Paul. "2006 College Construction Report," C2. The report is available at http://www.peterli.com/cpm/resources/rptscpm.shtm.

**Table 1.13** External and internal risks to consider

| External Risks (for example, related to donors or sponsors) | Internal Risks (for example, involving students or faculty) |
| --- | --- |
| **Economic** <br> • Availability of capital <br> • Debt rating <br> • Investment return <br> • Unemployment <br> • Interest rates <br> • Competition <br> **Environmental** <br> • Pollution control <br> • Ability to handle natural disasters <br> • Energy costs <br> • Waste disposal <br> **Political** <br> • Government regulations: federal, state, and local <br> • Legislative policies <br> • Public policy <br> • Neighborhood relations <br> **Social** <br> • Demographics <br> • Student and parent behavior <br> • Terrorism <br> • Privacy <br> **Technological** <br> • Emerging technology <br> • Data security <br> • Business interruptions | **Infrastructure** <br> • Availability of assets <br> • Access to capital <br> • Institutional structure: multicampus, international, and so forth <br> **Personnel** <br> • Employee capabilities <br> • Health and safety <br> • Organizational structure and decentralized responsibility <br> **Process** <br> • Formal policies and procedures <br> • Integration of key business functions <br> • Rigor of central administration and fiscal management <br> • Software and ERP implementation impact <br> **Technology** <br> • Data integrity <br> • System usability <br> • Usefulness of data <br> • System maintenance <br> **Compliance Matters** <br> • Accounting for sponsored projects <br> • NCAA rules and regulations <br> • Tax compliance <br> • Human subjects <br> • Scientific conduct |

## Impact of Policies on Costs

So far we have discussed cost trends that affect colleges and universities that are outside an institution's control. Another aspect to consider is the impact of an institution's policies—which boards typically establish—on its cost structure. For example, the board might approve a needs-blind financial aid policy, under which all entering first-year students are accepted without regard to need. This policy benefits society, giving those who are academically gifted but without financial resources the opportunity to attend the college of their choice, and it also benefits the institution, increasing the diversity of the stu-

dent body. However, it is an expensive policy. While the institution's mission and goals should guide the board's decision-making process, the board also must weigh the long-term financial implications of its policies. In later chapters, we will discuss costs that boards should control, since they can have a significant impact on an institution's financial condition.

## Risk

Board members should routinely consider risks, both internal and external to the institution. In 2004, the Committee of Sponsoring Organizations of the Treadway Commission (COSO) released *Enterprise Risk*

*Management—Integrated Framework,*[11] which explains how organizations can effectively identify and manage risk. For example, environmental risk—concerns about global warming and the increasing cost of energy—might require institutions to seek ways to adapt their physical plant to reduce energy consumption. Management must identify risks while the board must oversee a risk management program.

Colleges and universities face risks in many areas, including those summarized in Table 1.13. Using enterprise risk management (ERM) is important because it helps the board protect an institution's financial health. Many prominent colleges and universities have failed to manage risk effectively, resulting in multimillion-dollar fines and settlements related to misuse of federal grants or inappropriate billing for medical services. While ERM cannot guarantee such events will not occur, it reduces the chances of their happening.

## Key Questions

In the last section of this chapter, we suggest key questions for the board to ask as it reviews an institution's financial statements. (See Table 1.14.)

Of course, there are many other questions. Accreditation agencies, for example, require more financial information as part of their reaccreditation or approval of new programs. Asking tough questions and making sure the institution can answer them satisfactorily is one way the board satisfies its oversight responsibilities.

## Summary

Financial statements are a valuable resource for both internal and external users. From an internal perspective, college and university trustees need reliable financial information to make informed decisions. An

**Table 1.14** Representative key questions

| Issue | Questions |
|---|---|
| **Revenues** | · How dependent is the institution on each of its revenue sources? <br> · What steps can the institution take to diversify its revenue sources and reduce its dependence on any one source? |
| **Tuition and financial aid** | · Is institutional financial aid funded by external sources? <br> · What is the institution's effective discount on tuition? |
| **Endowment income** | · Is the institution striking the right risk/reward balance with its endowment funds to generate appropriate returns on its investments? |
| **Expenses** | · How much are expenses growing compared to revenues? <br> · Is the institution managing its expenses effectively? For example, has it investigated best practices for managing benefits costs? <br> · When setting policy, does the board consider the impact of its decisions on the institution's expenses? |
| **Salaries and benefits** | · Is the institution able to attract and retain top quality faculty and staff? <br> · How does its salary and benefits packages compare to those of its peers? |
| **Facilities** | · What capital requirements is the institution facing and what is its ability to raise the needed capital for facilities? <br> · Has the institution been deferring maintenance on its physical plant? <br> · Can the institution quantify its deferred maintenance? |
| **Intergenerational equity** | · In deliberations about revenues and costs, are board members considering how much of its resources the institution should preserve for future generations of students and how much it should spend for today's students? |

---

[11] For more information, see COSO's Web site at *http://www.coso.org.*

important source of such information is the institution's annual, independently audited financial statements and the notes that accompany them.[12] Audited financial statements also are a trusted resource for external users. For example, lenders and rating agencies often require colleges and universities to provide independently audited financial statements as terms of their debt agreements.

The board, especially the audit committee, needs to consider an institution's financial results within the context of the issues—like those cited in this chapter—that face higher education. It is not enough to look only at the numbers; the issues and trends behind the numbers are equally important.

In the next few chapters, we walk the reader through each financial statement, focusing on information used for board-level decisions. Our goal is to help trustees gain a new understanding of and appreciation for college and university financial statements and how to use them strategically to fulfill their board responsibilities.

---

12 Throughout this book, we make reference to "notes to the financial statements." They provide information about the accounting principles, judgments, and estimates used in preparing the financial statements.

# CHAPTER 2

# The Financial Reporting Process: Concepts and Definitions

Before we look at individual financial statements, we should discuss the concepts behind financial reporting. In this chapter, we look at the objectives and definitions that drive the process. In the next chapter, we focus on specific accounting requirements.

## Generally Accepted Accounting Principles

Receiving an unqualified, or clean, auditor's report is vital to a college or university's operations. Rating agencies, lenders, regulators, benefactors, and others often require an unqualified opinion before they can issue debt, award a grant, or process an institution's tax returns.

One of the requirements for an unqualified report is that an institution's financial statements follow "generally accepted accounting principles" (GAAP). This set of authoritative accounting standards outlines the minimum requirements for financial reporting, and it helps ensure that an institution's financial statements are reliable and complete. Moreover, financial statements that follow GAAP are easier to analyze when assessing an institution's financial health.

During an audit, the external independent auditor tests whether or not an institution has prepared its financial statements in accordance with GAAP. If the financial statements comply, the auditor includes the following paragraph in the report:

> In our opinion, the accompanying statement of financial position and the related statements of

activities, cash flows, and expenses by function present fairly, in all material respects, the financial position of [ABC University] at [date], and the changes in its net assets and its cash flows for the year then ended in conformity with accounting principles generally accepted in the United States of America.

Historically, GAAP was set by several bodies. However, in an effort to enhance the quality of financial reporting, the SEC recently named the Financial Accounting Standards Board (FASB) as the sole standard setting body. As a result, the FASB's "Hierarchy of Generally Accepted Accounting Principles" supersedes "Statement on Auditing Standards No. 69" from the American Institute of Certified Public Accountants (AICPA) entitled "The Meaning of Present Fairly in Conformity with Generally Accepted Accounting Principles." The FASB's new hierarchy applies to independent colleges, universities, not-for-profit organizations, and other entities that follow FASB pronouncements.[1]

## The Financial Reporting Process

In 1973 several accounting standards-setting bodies joined together to form the FASB. Its purpose is to establish guidelines that govern accounting practices in the United States. Through a series of statements, the FASB developed a conceptual framework for financial reporting, which underpins the foundation

---

[1] The FASB's new standards were adopted in May 2008.

for GAAP and helps guide decisions about accounting standards.

In this section, we highlight important concepts from the FASB's Statement of Financial Accounting Concepts (SFAC) No. 4, "Objectives of Financial Reporting by Nonbusiness Organizations," which defines the objectives of financial reporting, its key characteristics, the primary user groups, and its limitations.

**Objectives of financial reporting.** The FASB views financial reporting as a tool "to provide information that is useful in making decisions about allocating scarce resources."[2] Consequently, the primary objectives of financial reporting focus on the needs of resource providers. Their decisions to invest or not invest resources can affect significantly an institution's ability to meet its goals. The four objectives of financial reporting begin with a broad look at information about a college or university's financial standing and progressively narrow to the details.

The first objective is *to provide information that helps resource providers decide whether or not to allocate resources for the institution.* However, the FASB cautions that financial reporting does "not … determine what those decisions should be. The role of financial reporting requires it to provide neutral information."[3] In other words, financial reporting is not an answer; it is instead a way to evaluate information.

Interestingly, the FASB also makes it clear that good financial reporting requires commitment from both the preparers and readers of financial statements. "The information should be comprehensible to those who have a reasonable understanding of an organization's activities and are willing to study the information with reasonable diligence."[4] In other words, the college or university must provide clear and complete information, while the resource providers must understand the institution's purpose and know how to interpret financial statements.

The second objective of financial reporting is *to provide information that is useful in assessing an institution's services and its ability to continue providing them.* A good predictor of whether or not a college

or university successfully can provide services is its historical information. This objective recognizes that "expectations about future services of an organization … are based at least partly on evaluations of past performance. Thus, resource providers tend to direct their interest to information about the organization's resources and how it acquires and uses resources."[5] A wise institution will ensure that its financial reports clearly demonstrate how it managed resources.

The third objective of financial reporting is *to provide information that is useful in assessing how the institution's managers have executed their stewardship and other responsibilities.* Because colleges and universities do not have profit indicators, resource providers "must look to managers to represent their interests and to make operating cost/benefit judgments that achieve the objectives of the organization with minimum use of resources."[6] Financial reports should reflect managers' ability to use resources judiciously and comply with statutory and contractual obligations.

The FASB also recognizes that the success or failure of a college or university is due to numerous factors, and that the ability of its managers is only one of them. Other factors include events beyond the managers' control and the performance of past managers whose decisions affect future periods. Still, financial markets view the relative success of college and university managers as an indicator. Appointing individuals with the requisite management skills implies that the institution is more likely to use its resources effectively.

The final objective of financial reporting is *to provide information about the institution's economic resources, obligations, and net resources.* At this level of detail, resource providers are interested in transactions or events that have changed an institution's resources, its performance (via cash flows and program efforts and achievements), and liquidity. Resource providers "want to know how and why net resources changed during a period." This kind of information helps providers identify an institution's financial strengths and weaknesses and evaluate its performance and ability to continue providing services. Managers also can add explanations and interpretations that enhance the information.

---

2   Statement of Financial Accounting Concepts (SFAC) No. 4, par. 34.

3   Ibid.

4   Ibid., par. 35.

5   Ibid., par. 39.

6   Ibid., par. 40.

In summary, financial reporting should provide information to meet the common interests of external resource providers and other users. The information should help individuals:

+ Make rational decisions about the institution's allocation of resources;

+ Assess its services and ability to continue providing them;

+ Evaluate its managers' performance as stewards of the institution's resources; and

+ Analyze its economic resources and obligations.

**Key characteristics.** The FASB defines useful information as both relevant and reliable. "Relevant" information has the characteristics of predictive value, feedback value, and timeliness. In other words, financial reporting not only reviews past events, it also indicates the future state of the institution. For example, when external users consider lending money to an institution, they use relevant information to determine if the college or university is financially viable. "Reliable" information is verifiable, faithful in its representation, and neutral. In other words, the user should be able to trust that the information, as presented, captures the economic reality of the institution.

There is often conflict between relevance and reliability. If users want totally reliable information, they often must wait until the outcome is known. However, the information may lose its relevance, as it would not be timely. An example would be a financial contingency facing the institution. While the exact outcome might not be known for some time, the materiality of the contingency might be relevant to the users and timely in their decision-making process. Therefore, it is important to remember that financial reporting includes estimates and accounting choices that can affect the quality of its information.

**Primary user groups.** Underlying the conceptual framework are the needs of the users of financial information. The FASB defines four major groups:

> *Resource providers* include those who are directly compensated for providing resources—lenders, suppliers, and employees—and those who are not directly and proportionately compensated—

members, contributors, and taxpayers. *Constituents* are those who use and benefit from the services rendered by the organization. *Governing and oversight bodies* are those responsible for setting policies and for overseeing and appraising managers of nonbusiness organizations. *Managers* of an organization are responsible for carrying out the policy mandates of governing bodies and managing the day-to-day operations of an organization.[7]

These four groups share a common interest in the college or university. They want to know about its effectiveness in providing services, and its ability to continue doing so. For example, contributors may use the institution's financial reports to make decisions about their continued support. Lenders want to know whether the college or university can meet its debt service. Governing boards use financial reports to help them decide whether they should change any institutional policies; they also use them as a performance indicator for the managers. Financial reports must address the needs of all the different users.

The FASB makes special note of "internal users"—managers and, sometimes, governing boards—who "need a great deal of internal accounting information to carry out their responsibilities in planning and controlling activities."[8] Examples of specialized information include "[evaluation of] competing funding requests for capital projects … [and] compliance with spending mandates established by budgetary appropriations or donor or grantor restrictions."[9] The detail required for such decisions is necessarily tailored to the specific institution and therefore goes beyond the scope of the FASB's conceptual framework.

**Limitations.** In both the for-profit and not-for-profit sectors, financial reporting is based on significant estimates and judgments. It is not an exact science. Therefore changes in estimates affect how external users may interpret an institution's reports. For example, colleges and universities must use estimates in depreciating assets and estimating collectibility of accounts receivable and pledges.

---

[7]  Ibid., par. 29.

[8]  Ibid., par. 32.

[9]  Ibid.

**Table 2.1** Definitions of the seven elements of financial statements

- **Assets** are items that an organization owns or controls and that have the potential to be of service or future economic benefit. They are the results of past transactions. Examples include cash, investments, property, plant, and equipment.
- **Liabilities** are sacrifices of economic benefit. They are future payments—or other obligations—of an organization resulting from a past transaction. For example, "using employees' knowledge, skills, time, and efforts obligates an [organization] to pay for their use, often including fringe benefits."† Other examples include accounts payable and long-term debt.
- **Net assets** are the difference between an organization's assets and liabilities. For-profit businesses use the term "equity" for this same concept. Not-for-profit net assets are classified as permanently restricted, temporarily restricted, or unrestricted.
- **Revenues** are inflows resulting from the provision of services or other activities related to an organization's operations. They increase an organization's assets. Examples include tuition revenue and investment income.
- **Expenses** are cash outflows caused by the production or delivery of an organization's goods and services. They also can be incurrences of liabilities. Examples include instruction, academic support, and administration.
- **Gains** are increases in net assets caused by transactions outside the organization's operations. An example would be the settlement from a lawsuit. Gains may be classified as either operating or non-operating.
- **Losses** are decreases in net assets caused by transactions outside the organization's operations. An example would be damage to the campus caused by a natural disaster. As with gains, losses also may be classified as either operating or non-operating.

*Source:* FASB, "Elements of Financial Statements," SFAC no. 6 (December 1985), *http://www.fasb.org/st.*
†SFAC No. 6, par. 38.

As an information system, financial reporting should be a good indicator of future activities and cash flows for making decisions. However, financial reporting reflects only events that have already occurred; it makes no predictions about future performance. Moreover, financial reporting provides only one kind of information to users. Economic, social, and political information from other sources may be equally important in evaluating an institution's performance.

Although the FASB notes many similarities between the financial reporting of for-profit and not-for-profit entities, they differ in how they obtain resources.[10] Those who provide resources to not-for-profit organizations do so not for economic benefits but rather because they wish to further the organization's mission-specific goals. However, resource providers and/or governing boards frequently specify how a not-for-profit organization can spend its resources. Usually, restrictions take one of two forms: donors restrict their gifts, or the nature of the organization specifies

its budgetary appropriations for a particular use.

There is an additional limitation on the financial reports of not-for-profit organizations. The external market helps measure the quality of business enterprises' goods and services by reflecting profits or losses in their stock prices. Not-for-profit organizations have no such objective, external market indicators. However, there is an increased emphasis on accountability by many external constituents, and they use financial reports as a way to assess the financial viability of these organizations.

# Elements of Financial Statements

In this section, we review the FASB's "Elements of Financial Statements" (SFAC No. 6), which defines seven elements of financial reporting: assets, liabilities, net assets, revenues, expenses, gains, and losses. Because net assets are unique to not-for-profit organizations, we examine them in detail.

---

[10]  The FASB notes that budgets also play an important role in obtaining resources for not-for-profit organizations. For example, college and university budgets are used to help set tuition levels. Although budgets are not required for external financial reporting, they are integral to an organization's planning process and provide feedback on how the organization met its budget expectations.

**Definitions.** Elements are the building blocks of financial statements. They "refer to broad classes, such as assets, liabilities, revenues, and expenses," that measure the performance and status of an organization.[11] Table 2.1 provides definitions for the seven elements that pertain to not-for-profits.

**Net assets.** The three categories of net assets are (1) permanently restricted net assets, (2) temporarily restricted net assets, and (3) unrestricted net assets. The key distinction among the three classes is the institution's degree of control over their use.

With permanently restricted net assets, the institution is bound by outside resource providers—donors, for example—who require the institution to retain their gifts indefinitely. True endowment funds are permanently restricted, as they are gifts made by donors who have specified that the principal (and sometimes a portion of its accumulated income) may not be spent.[12]

With temporarily restricted net assets, donors (or resource providers) require the institution to use the gift for a specific purpose and after a period of time has transpired or after the institution fulfills a donor-stipulated action. Temporarily restricted net assets include:

+ Principally, the realized and unrealized gains on the institution's permanent endowment whose use the donor has restricted for specific purposes;

+ Unexpended endowment income or current gifts for which the institution has not satisfied the donors' restrictions; and

+ Contributions receivable in future periods that ultimately may be used to support operations. Because the amounts are not yet available, they are listed as temporarily restricted net assets.

In the case of unrestricted net assets, the institution has full control over the use of the net assets. Principally, all revenue and expense activity, with the exception of certain contribution and investment activity, flows through unrestricted net assets. However, not

all unrestricted net assets are used for operating costs. For example, institution managers or boards may designate unrestricted net assets for net investment in plant; specific current or future needs of the institution; or quasi endowment funds, which are board-designated funds to be invested as part of the institution's endowment.[13]

The three categories of net assets are similar to the stockholders' equity section in a for-profit financial statement. In other words, readers can view:

+ Permanently restricted net assets as similar to common stock;

+ Unrestricted net assets as similar to retained earnings; and

+ Temporarily restricted net assets as having characteristics of both common stocks and retained earnings.

The separation of net assets into these three categories captures an institution's flexibility in using its funds, an important indicator for the financial markets.

## Summary

The FASB's Statements of Financial Accounting Concepts provide the rationale behind GAAP standards. They define terms and make clear the purpose of financial reporting. It is important for board members to keep these issues in mind as they review college and university financial statements.

In the next chapter, we delve into the standards themselves and the FASB's expectations of not-for-profit organizations in their financial reporting.

---

[11]  SFAC No. 6, par. 5, "Elements of Financial Statements."

[12]  In certain states—Rhode Island, for example—the laws also may require that a portion of the realized and unrealized gains on endowment investments be added to permanently restricted net assets to preserve that capital against the effects of inflation.

---

[13]  The amounts invested at the board's discretion can be either current unrestricted or restricted resources.

# CHAPTER 3

# The Financial Reporting Process: Standards

As the standard-setting body for accounting, the FASB issues statements that define financial reporting practices. In the previous chapter, we explored two statements of financial concepts that explain the conceptual framework behind financial reporting—the objectives, the users, and the characteristics. A second set of FASB statements focuses on accounting standards. They detail requirements for financial reporting, essentially providing the rules that all businesses—for-profit and not-for-profit alike—must follow to comply with GAAP.

In this chapter, then, we look at two statements of financial accounting standards (SFAS) that affect colleges and universities. They are SFAS No. 116, "Accounting for Contributions Received and Contributions Made," and SFAS No. 117, "Financial Statements of Not-for-Profit Organizations."

## Contributions Received and Made

While for-profits and not-for-profits follow many of the same accounting practices, not-for-profits receive contributions, which require special attention. SFAS No. 116 outlines the accounting of contributions received and made, including whether an item qualifies as a contribution and how to record it in the financial statements.

**Types of contributions.** "Unconditional contributions" are voluntary, nonreciprocal contributions to a college or university. They can be either an asset, such as a monetary or in-kind donation, or a reduction of

liability, such as the cancellation of an obligation. Institutions should record the unconditional contributions they receive at their fair values as revenues or gains in the period received and as assets (or decreases in liabilities or expenses). Their classification as permanently restricted, temporarily restricted, or unrestricted net assets depends on the donor's requirements.

Many colleges and universities also receive "pledges," or unconditional promises to give, which they should recognize as revenue (equal to the net present value of the amounts expected to be received/realized) as long as verifiable documentation exists. A pledge with payments due in future periods should be reported as restricted support, unless the donor indicates the pledge as supporting current operations. SFAS No. 116 requires institutions to provide detailed information about their pledges in the notes to the financial statements.

"Conditional promises to give" are when donors require a specific event or action to occur before they transfer an asset. If the institution fails to meet the conditions, donors have the right to withdraw their promise to give. Colleges and universities should report conditional promises to give when they substantially meet the conditions on which the pledges depend. If a donor's stipulations are ambiguous, the institution should presume the pledge is a conditional promise to give.

**Contributed services.** Some institutions may receive services, such as volunteer labor, from donors instead of cash gifts. They should recognize contributed services that (1) create or enhance nonfinancial assets, or (2) are provided by individuals with specialized skills that would otherwise require purchase.[1] As with pledges, the FASB requires institutions to explain the nature of any contributed services received in the notes to the financial statements. The explanations should reflect the expenses the institution would have incurred if the services had not been donated.

**Collections.** Some colleges and universities have museums, collections of art, or other collectible items. Institutions do not need to recognize collections in their financial statements if they meet all of the following conditions:

+ The collectible items are held for public exhibition, education, or research to further public service;

+ They are protected, kept unencumbered, cared for, and preserved; and

+ They are subject to an organizational policy that requires the proceeds from the sale of a collectible item be used to acquire other items for the collection.

If the collectible items do not meet all of these conditions, the institution must capitalize and record them in the financial statements. If collectible items are contributed, the college or university should report them as revenues or gains at the verifiable value of the items.

**Contributions made.** SFAS No. 116 also applies to for-profit entities that may make contributions. For-profit and not-for-profit organizations should record their donations to other entities as an expense in the period made and as a decrease of assets or increase of liabilities, depending on the form of the contribution. Likewise, colleges and universities should record a pledge as an expense with an accompanying liability until they fulfill it.

# Financial Statements

In SFAS No. 117, the FASB aligns financial reporting in the not-for-profit sector with that of the for-profit sector. Colleges and universities must present three financial statements: a statement of financial position, a statement of activities, and a statement of cash flows.

Together, they provide users with the information necessary to assess an institution's financial condition and evaluate its success in executing its mission. Colleges and universities that develop statements in compliance with SFAS No. 117 meet the growing demand for accountability, which in turn strengthens their positions to continue receiving support from various resource providers.

**Statement of financial position.** The statement of financial position (also called the balance sheet) focuses on the organization as a whole, presenting the institution's assets, liabilities, and net assets for a given time period.

The statement of financial position provides information about "(a) the organization's ability to continue to provide services and (b) the organization's liquidity, financial flexibility, ability to meet obligations, and needs for external financing."[2] Liquidity is the institution's ability to meet its current obligations and cover its expenses, essentially a current view of the institution's cash needs. Financial flexibility represents the organization's ability to respond to changes in its longer-term cash needs and to incur debt if needed.

To reflect liquidity, colleges and universities should use one of the following methods:

+ Classifying assets as current and noncurrent;

+ Sequencing assets and liabilities according to liquidity; or

+ Disclosing relevant information about liquidity in the notes.

In the statement of financial position, colleges and universities must classify their net assets as permanently restricted, temporarily restricted, or unrestricted, based on definitions provided in SFAC No. 6. (See "Net assets" in Chapter 2.) Institutions can also disclose self-imposed limitations (such as quasi endowment or amounts designated for other specified areas) either in the notes or on the face of the statement.

**Statement of activities.** The statement of activities (also called the income statement) provides information about the changes in the three classes

---

[1] Many volunteer services do not meet these requirements and, therefore, are not recorded as contributed services.

[2] SFAS No. 117, par. 9.

of net assets and how the institution has used them to provide services during the previous year. This information should assist donors and creditors in evaluating the institution's performance, its service efforts, and its success in executing its stewardship responsibilities.[3]

At a minimum, the statement of activities must report the changes in each of the three classes of net assets and total net assets for the period. An institution can report a "measure of operations," which is similar to the for-profit sector's "net income from continuing operations." This measure relates revenues and expenses, so users can determine if the college or university is operating within its means. If such a measure is provided, the statement of activities must still include the total change in unrestricted net assets for the period (which might include nonoperating activity, such as gifts or transfers of net assets from temporarily restricted net assets). As long as an institution meets the minimum requirements, it may classify items "as operating and nonoperating, expendable and nonexpendable, earned and unearned, recurring and nonrecurring, or in other ways."[4]

The statement of activities—in particular the column for unrestricted net assets—is basically the institution's income statement. It provides information about a college or university's operations: the costs of various programs and the institution's ability to use its available resources judiciously.

**Statement of cash flows.**[5] The statement of cash flows provides information about an institution's cash receipts and cash payments. Like for-profit entities, not-for-profit organizations segregate their activities into three categories on the statement of cash flows: cash flows from operations, investing, and financing activities. Cash flows from operations indicates whether or not the institution is receiving cash from its operating activities. Investing cash flows reports the purchase or sale of investments, property, plant, and equipment. Financing cash flows reflects the issu-

ance and/or repayment of debt as well as proceeds from contributions. Financing activities may include "receipts from contributions and investment income that by donor stipulation are restricted for the purposes of acquiring, constructing, or improving property, plant, equipment, or other long-lived assets or establishing or increasing a permanent endowment or term endowment."[6]

The cash flow statement allows users to assess a college or university's ability to meet its ongoing cash needs from operations or through other forms of financing. For example, if cash flows from operations are negative, the institution will need to meet this deficit through additional contribution or borrowing activity.

## Summary

Good financial reporting is critical to a college or university's success. It is central to accreditation, bond market ratings, and applications for federal student aid, and it is required when seeking funds from foundations and donors. Financial reports should reflect the institution's mission and strategic goals and relay how successful the institution has been in this regard. With the external public's increasing demand for accountability, colleges and universities should use financial reports to document their management of resources.

In *Reinventing the University: Managing and Financing Institutions of Higher Education*, Robert M. Turner and Kenneth D. Williams note "the standard setting bodies have provided the not-for-profit industry with the opportunity to play a major role in how methods of accountability and evaluation develop. Those institutions that actively play a role in this process will be able to develop meaningful systems of reporting that not only enhance external financial reports, but also those internal reports that are critical to carrying out their managerial and governing responsibilities effectively."[7]

In the following chapters, we examine the three primary financial statements.

---

[3]  Ibid., par. 17.

[4]  Ibid., par. 23.

[5]  SFAS No. 117 amends SFAS No. 95 "Statement of Cash Flows," extending its provisions to not-for-profit organizations, including colleges and universities. The terms "statement of activities" and "change in net assets" apply to a not-for-profit organization; the terms "income statement" and "net income" apply to a business enterprise.

[6]  SFAS No. 117, par. 30.

[7]  Turner and Williams, "Greater Accountability in Financial Reporting," (New York: John Wiley and Sons, Inc., 1995).

# CHAPTER 4

# Statement of Financial Position

The statement of financial position, or balance sheet, is a snapshot of an institution's financial condition at a particular point in time, generally the end of the fiscal year. This statement should provide users with information about an institution's ongoing ability to provide services and information on its liquidity, financial flexibility, and financing needs.[1]

Statements of financial position must display the following:

1. Total assets

2. Total liabilities

3. Total net assets

4. Totals for each of the three classes of net assets: unrestricted, temporarily restricted, and permanently restricted

Most institutions aggregate each type of asset and liability to present their financial statements in a highly condensed and meaningful format, similar to that of a for-profit enterprise. Cash, for example, is often presented as a single, total amount rather than separated by fund; a single entry for investments provides a clear picture of the institution's resources. Likewise, aggregating liabilities succinctly presents the institution's total obligations, both short-term and long-term.

Of special note in the assets are net contributions receivable (or pledges). Following requirements outlined in SFAS No. 116, institutions must list the net amount of their unconditional pledges, deducting from the total pledges that are unlikely to be paid.

As discussed in Chapter 3, institutions reflect the liquidity of their assets and liabilities in three ways: (1) by clas-

sifying assets as current or noncurrent; (2) by sequencing assets according to their nearness of conversion to cash and liabilities according to their nearness to requiring the use of cash; or (3) by disclosing information about liquidity in the notes to the financial statements. SanJo University, our illustrative model for this book, uses the second method, sequencing items by liquidity.

In listing their net assets, colleges and universities may provide varying degrees of detail on each class, with appropriate explanation either in the notes to the financial statements or on the statement itself. (See Chapter 2 for definitions and examples of each class of net assets.)

## Reading the Statement of Financial Position for SanJo University

Exhibit A shows the statement of financial position for our hypothetical institution, SanJo University. It displays the assets, liabilities, and the net assets of the institution in a fairly simple and understandable format.[2]

The statement of financial position for SanJo University presents fiscal year (FY) 2007 and FY 2006 information, the latter providing a basis for comparison. The three categories—assets, liabilities, and net assets—are highlighted in bold. Exhibit A shows SanJo has total assets of $812,533, total liabilities of $124,893, and total net assets of $687,640 at the end of FY 2007. The university's net assets

---

[1] SFAS No. 117, par. 9.

[2] Throughout this book the numbers for the financial statements in both the tables and the running text are expressed in thousands. That is, $341,413 actually is $341,413,000. We have dropped the zeros in the interest of readability.

**Exhibit A** SanJo University statement of financial position, FY 2007 and FY 2006

**SanJo University**
**Statement of Financial Position**

For the two years ended June 30, 2007 and 2006
(in thousands)

| | 2007 | 2006 |
|---|---|---|
| **Assets** | | |
| Cash and cash equivalents | $14,200 | $14,225 |
| Accounts receivable, net | 1,700 | 1,650 |
| Short-term investments | 10,925 | 10,850 |
| Inventories | 1,380 | 1,325 |
| Prepaid expenses and other assets | 2,518 | 2,425 |
| Pledges receivable, net | 168,214 | 210,875 |
| Student loans receivable, net | 4,131 | 3,592 |
| Long-term investments, at market | 416,466 | 301,961 |
| Land, buildings, and equipment, net | 192,999 | 175,000 |
| Total assets | $812,533 | $721,903 |
| | | |
| **Liabilities** | | |
| Accounts payable and accrued expenses | $8,977 | $7,800 |
| Deposits and deferred revenues | 4,760 | 4,033 |
| Postretirement benefits | 9,799 | 8,548 |
| Federal student loan funds | 4,106 | 3,544 |
| Long-term debt | 97,251 | 85,479 |
| Total liabilities | $124,893 | $109,404 |
| | | |
| **Net assets** | | |
| Unrestricted | | |
| Funds functioning as endowment | $79,079 | $77,874 |
| Investment in plant, net of long-term debt | 95,748 | 89,521 |
| Undesignated | 24,373 | 16,019 |
| Unrestricted total | 199,200 | 183,414 |
| Temporarily restricted | 103,976 | 99,912 |
| Permanently restricted | 384,464 | 329,173 |
| Total net assets | $687,640 | $612,499 |
| | | |
| Total liabilities and net assets | $812,533 | $721,903 |

include unrestricted net assets of $199,200, temporarily restricted net assets of $103,976, and permanently restricted net assets of $384,464.

Note 7 of SanJo's financial statements details the composition of the university's net assets. (See Appendix A.) The unrestricted net assets of $199,200 include $24,373 labeled as "Undesignated – available for operating needs." These funds could be used for basic working capital needs or other institutional needs as identified by the board and/or management (for example, deferred maintenance, program support, and construction projects). Its unrestricted net assets also include the $79,079 unrestricted portion of the endowment fund ("Funds functioning as endowment") and the institution's $95,748 net investment in its physical plant.

SanJo's temporarily restricted net assets of $103,976 include $56,792 for "Amounts restricted by donors for specific purposes," which may include items such as unexpended restricted gifts and unexpended endowment income. The other categories include $39,211 of "Accumulated gains on permanent endowment whose income is donor restricted" and $7,973 of "Pledges receivable for specific purposes" that will eventually be available for use.

The permanently restricted net assets total $384,464 and include $224,223 of "Permanent endowment and similar funds" and $160,241 of "Pledges for permanent endowment." By definition, the only portion of the endowment that is included here is the original corpus of gifts plus any income or gains that the donor—or state law—has mandated be added to the corpus. Pledges listed here represent amounts that upon receipt will become part of the corpus of the endowment fund.

## Analyzing the Statement of Financial Position

The main strategic question boards should ask when reviewing a statement of financial position is: *Does the institution have enough resources to fulfill its mission?*

A relatively simple indicator of an institution's financial strength is the growth in net assets and in each category of net assets. Table 4.1 shows SanJo's net assets increased overall as well as in almost every category from 2006 to 2007. This growth suggests the university is in a relatively strong financial position.

The statement of financial position helps board members evaluate the financial condition of an institution by answering questions such as:

- What are the net assets worth?
- Will the institution be able to pay its debts?
- Can the institution afford to provide students with need-blind financial aid?
- How reliant is the institution on debt to support its activities?
- Does the institution have enough resources to fulfill its mission?

Ultimately, a good statement of financial position provides readers with a summary of an institution's financial health. It shows what the college or university has (assets), what it owes (liabilities), and what is left (net assets). Together, this information indicates the college or university's liquidity, financial flexibility, and financing needs, all of which influence the institution's ability to provide services.

In Chapter 7 we return to the statement of financial position, using ratio analysis to explore various dimensions of the university's financial strength.

**Table 4.1** Analyzing the composition of net assets (from Appendix A, Note 7)

| | 2007 | 2006 | Change % |
|---|---|---|---|
| **Unrestricted net assets** | | | |
| Undesignated – available for operating needs | $24,373 | $16,019 | 52.2 |
| Funds functioning as endowment and accumulated gains on permanent endowment whose income is unrestricted[a] | 79,079 | 77,874 | 1.5 |
| Investment In plant, net of long-term debt | 95,748 | 89,521 | 7.0 |
| | $199,200 | $183,414 | 8.6 |
| **Temporarily restricted net assets** | | | |
| Accumulated gains on permanent endowment whose income is restricted[a] | 39,211 | 36,911 | 6.2 |
| Amounts restricted by donors for specific purposes | 56,792 | 57,126 | -0.6 |
| Pledges receivable for specific purposes | 7,973 | 5,875 | 35.7 |
| | $103,976 | $99,912 | 4.1 |
| **Permanently restricted net assets** | | | |
| Permanent endowment and similar funds[a] | 224,223 | 124,173 | 80.6 |
| Pledges for permanent endowment[a] | 160,241 | 205,000 | 21.9 |
| | $384,464 | $329,173 | 16.8 |
| **Total net assets** | $687,640 | $612,499 | 12.3 |
| [a]The sum of these items equals Total Endowment | $502,754 | $443,958 | |

# CHAPTER 5

# Statement of Activities

The statement of activities—also called the income statement—presents aggregated information about an institution's revenues, expenses, and other sources of funds. The FASB requires the statement of activities to:

♦ Report the total changes in each class of net assets (unrestricted, temporarily restricted, and permanently restricted net assets);

♦ Show the total changes in all net assets for the period; and

♦ Show all expenses as being expended from unrestricted net assets. If a college or university uses temporarily restricted net assets to meet current expenses, it must present that the resources were released from restrictions and reclassified as unrestricted.

One of the most significant differences between for-profit and not-for-profit entities is the manner in which they present their operating results. For-profit enterprises present an income statement, which focuses on what happened during the fiscal year to generate its net income or loss. Not-for-profit organizations, however, must distinguish between the changes in net assets that result from operations and those that do not (such as capital transactions).[1] As such, many colleges and universities manage their financial affairs by establishing an operating budget and measuring their operating performance against it.

The important point here is that colleges and universities essentially have two bottom lines on their statements of activities; one for changes in operating net assets and another for changes in total net assets.

The statement of activities captures information about the operating activity of an institution, its investment management results, and its fundraising activities. Therefore, the four major areas most institutions will want to measure in their income statements are overall results, operating results, investment performance, and fundraising results. There are, of course, other areas that may be significant in any given year.

Because the FASB did not prescribe a single format for the statement of activities, colleges and universities have used many different ones. The format the institution chooses can disguise or emphasize different performance measures. At the end of this chapter, we discuss the three formats most commonly found in college and university financial reports.

## Reading the Statement of Activities for SanJo University

Exhibit B shows the statement of activities for SanJo University. The statement contains four columns for FY 2007 (Unrestricted, Temporarily Restricted, Permanently Restricted, and 2007 Totals) and, for comparison, another column for FY 2006 Totals. SanJo's statement of activities has three sections—Operating Revenues, Operating Expenses, and Non-operat-

---

[1] Institutions may choose to report a "measure of operations," which compares revenues and expenses. While the FASB does not require the inclusion of measures of operation, it does require a college or university to make clear what is included or excluded from them. Most institutions accomplish this in the first section of the notes to the financial statements, Summary of Significant Accounting Policies.

**Exhibit B** SanJo University statement of activities, FY 2007 and FY 2006

**SanJo University**
**Statement of Activities**

For the two years ended June 30, 2007 and 2006 (in thousands)

| | Unrestricted | Temporarily restricted | Permanently restricted | Totals 2007 | 2006 |
|---|---|---|---|---|---|
| **Operating revenues** | | | | | |
| Tuition and fees | $66,300 | | | $66,300 | $62,985 |
| University-sponsored financial aid | (10,294) | | | (10,294) | (9,347) |
| Donor-sponsored financial aid | (11,562) | | | (11,562) | (11,000) |
| Net tuition and fees | 44,444 | | | 44,444 | 42,638 |
| Sales and services of auxiliaries | 14,807 | | | 14,807 | 14,101 |
| Government grants and contracts | 2,750 | | | 2,750 | 2,633 |
| Private gifts and grants | 5,436 | 3,672 | | 9,108 | 8,279 |
| Investment income used for operations | 13,594 | | | 13,594 | 12,569 |
| Other income | 1,750 | | | 1,750 | 1,590 |
| Net assets released from restrictions | 1,908 | (1,908) | | | |
| Total operating revenues | $84,689 | $1,764 | | $86,453 | $81,810 |
| **Operating expenses** | | | | | |
| Instruction and research | 37,062 | | | 37,062 | 35,090 |
| Libraries | 4,401 | | | 4,401 | 3,972 |
| Academic support | 7,852 | | | 7,852 | 7,398 |
| Student services | 7,504 | | | 7,504 | 7,070 |
| General administration | 13,132 | | | 13,132 | 12,372 |
| Auxiliaries enterprises | 12,357 | | | 12,357 | 11,642 |
| Total operating expenses | $82,308 | | | $82,308 | $77,544 |
| Increase in net assets from operating activities | $2,381 | $1,764 | | $4,145 | $4,266 |
| **Nonoperating activities** | | | | | |
| Total investment income | 8,207 | 6,892 | | 15,099 | 7,684 |
| Less investment income used for operations | (9,002) | (4,592) | | (13,594) | (12,569) |
| Capital gifts | 2,000 | 10,000 | 55,291 | 67,291 | 159,411 |
| Other | 2,200 | | | 2,200 | (5,884) |
| Net assets released from restrictions | 10,000 | (10,000) | | | |
| Increase in net assets from nonoperating activities | $13,405 | $2,300 | $55,291 | $70,996 | $148,642 |
| Net increase in net assets | 15,786 | 4,064 | 55,291 | 75,141 | 152,908 |
| Net assets at beginning of year | 183,414 | 99,912 | 329,173 | 612,499 | 459,591 |
| Net assets at end of year | $199,200 | $103,976 | $384,464 | $687,640 | $612,499 |

ing Activities—which are indicated in bold on the statement.

Reading across the statement of activities, the total unrestricted operating revenues for FY 2007 are $84,689; temporarily restricted operating revenues are $1,764; and there are no permanently restricted operating revenues. The total operating revenues, then, for FY 2007 are $86,453. Similarly, total unrestricted operating expenses are $82,308. Because GAAP requires that all operating expenses come from unrestricted net assets, there are no temporarily or permanently restricted operating expenses.

Immediately following the operating expenses is "Increase in net assets from operating activities," which is the measure of operations that SanJo University has chosen. Unrestricted operations increased $2,381 and temporarily restricted activities increased $1,764 for a total increase of $4,145 for FY 2007.

The "Increase in net assets from non-operating activities" is another measure of operations. As required by the FASB, SanJo explains its definitions for the measures of operations in Note 1(a), Summary of Significant Accounting Policies: Basis of Presentation. (See Appendix B.)

"Net increase in net assets" applies to each of the three net asset classes and measures the total change in net worth (or, in for-profit terms, equity). For SanJo University the total 2007 increase in net assets is $75,141, which includes increases in unrestricted net assets of $15,786, temporarily restricted net assets of $4,064, and permanently restricted net assets of $55,291.

Finally, the total change in net assets for each of the three net asset categories is added to the "Net assets at beginning of year" to determine the year-end values of the net assets by category. These year end totals should correspond to the totals for each category in the "Net assets" section of the Statement of Financial Position. (See Exhibit A.)

## Analyzing the Statement of Activities

The fundamental question the statement of activities answers is "How well did the institution use its resources to provide services to its constituents?" To evaluate this broad question, we recommend the following eight questions and their indicators and consideration factors. This list is merely a starting point. Board members and administrators should add their own questions tailored to the institution's unique mission.

1. **Overall, how did SanJo University perform financially for the year?** This question takes a broad perspective of the university's financial performance for the year.

   *Indicators.* The following indicators are based on "Net increase in net assets" as one measure of the university's financial performance.

   - "Net increase in net assets" as a percentage of the "Net assets at beginning of year" (Indicator A)

   - "Net increase in unrestricted net assets" as a percentage of the "Unrestricted net assets at beginning of year" (Indicator B)

   - "Net increase in temporarily restricted net assets" as a percentage of the "Temporarily restricted net assets at beginning of year" (Indicator C)

   - "Net increase in permanently restricted net assets" as a percentage of the "Permanently restricted net assets at beginning of year" (Indicator D)

*Factors to consider*

- Net assets should increase at a rate exceeding inflation and, hopefully, at a much quicker pace if the institution is to achieve real growth. An increase in net assets enhances the financial strength of the institution because the net assets provide the institution with financial flexibility.

- Unrestricted and permanently restricted net assets are especially important and should increase at a rate exceeding inflation. Temporarily restricted net assets are less important, because they reflect assets that are restricted only for a period of time or for a donor-specified purpose. They are more likely to fluctuate from one period to the next.

*Analysis.* The university's "Net increase in net assets" for the year was $75,141, or 12.3 percent of "Net assets at beginning of year," which was $612,499. (See Indicator A on Table 5.1.) In addition, each of the three net asset categories showed growth. (See indicators B, C, and D on Table 5.1.) In all cases, the level of growth exceeded that of inflation, which was roughly 3 percent for the period. These FY 2007 increases in net assets for SanJo University enhance its financial strength.

**Table 5.1** Increase in net assets for SanJo University

| Net asset category | Increase in net assets | Net assets beginning of year | Percent increase | |
|---|---|---|---|---|
| Unrestricted | $15,786 | $183,414 | 8.6 | **(B)** |
| Temporarily restricted | 4,064 | 99,912 | 4.1 | **(C)** |
| Permanently restricted | 55,291 | 329,173 | 16.8 | **(D)** |
| Total | $75,141 | $612,499 | 12.3 | **(A)** |

2. **Is SanJo University living within its means?** This question considers whether the university is able to meet its operating expenses with its operating revenues.

*Indicator.* Increase or decrease in unrestricted net assets from operating activities.

*Factors to consider*

+ A net increase from operating activities indicates the institution's operating revenues exceeded its expenses, and the institution is living within its means.

+ A college or university may channel an operating surplus into long-term reinvestment in the institution if the board designates certain funds for quasi endowment or for the physical plant.

+ If an institution is not living within its means, it must find a way to meet the deficit in the short term and create a surplus in future years.

**Table 5.2** Change in unrestricted net assets from operating activities

| Line item | 2007 Totals |
|---|---|
| Total unrestricted operating revenues | $84,689 |
| Total unrestricted operating expenses | $82,308 |
| Increase in unrestricted net assets from operating activities | $2,381 |

Another important question is "Did the institution live within its budget?" In the past, many institutions have not budgeted in a manner consistent with their external financial reports; for example, they may not have included depreciation as a budgeted expense. Therefore, trustees should compare the reported operating surplus or deficit (measure of operations) to the institution's budget.

*Analysis.* Table 5.2 shows that SanJo University's operating revenue in FY 2007 exceeded its operating expenses, so the university appears to be living within its means.

3. **How reliant is the institution on each of its operating revenue sources?** This question considers the diversity and breadth of the university's revenue stream.

*Indicator.* Each operating revenue source (tuition and fees, private gifts and grants, and so forth) as a percentage of total operating revenues.

*Factors to consider*

+ Although it may seem obvious, it is important to recognize that the broader an institution's revenue streams, the less exposure it has to risk resulting from fluctuations in any one source.

+ Each revenue source may have a different life cycle. For example, tuition revenues usually operate in two-year or four-year cycles (for two-year and four-year programs); research revenues generally operate in cycles corresponding to the terms of major contracts and grants; and endowment income operates in perpetuity. The mix of short-term and long-term revenue sources and the volatility of each source can be important when considering new long-term commitments.

*Analysis.* Table 5.3 shows that 52.4 percent of the university's revenue comes from tuition and fees, indicating SanJo depends heavily on such revenue (although many independent institutions rely even more on tuition and fees than our fictitious university). The university will need to monitor this tuition dependence and seek other sustainable revenue sources to reduce it.

**Table 5.3** The university's dependence on operating revenue sources

| Operating revenues | 2007 Totals | % of Total revenue |
|---|---|---|
| Net tuition and fees | $44,444 | 52.4 |
| Sales and services of auxiliaries | 14,807 | 17.5 |
| Government grants and contracts | 2,750 | 3.2 |
| Private gifts and grants | 5,436 | 6.4 |
| Investment income used for operations | 13,594 | 16.1 |
| Other income | 1,750 | 2.1 |
| Net assets released from restrictions | 1,908 | 2.3 |
| Total operating revenue | $84,689 | 100.0 |

4. **Do operating expenses by cost category (instruction, institutional support, and so forth) reflect institutional priorities?** This question considers whether the institution's spending patterns reflect its mission.

*Indicator.* Each operating expense as a percentage of total operating revenue.

*Factors to consider*

♦ Instruction is central to the mission of most colleges and universities. Consequently, instructional expenses should be as high as possible in relation to total expenses. Institutions should also assess instructional expenses as a percentage of total operating expenses and instructional expenses per full-time equivalent (FTE) student.

♦ Similarly, many institutions want to minimize institutional support expenses (such as legal costs, fiscal operations, general administrative services, purchasing, security, development, and community relations), maintaining or improving service but at a lower cost. Institutional support expenses should be held in check relative to total expenses.

♦ A board will generally want to shift operating expenses over time to reflect changing institutional priorities. Also, the board may decide to focus on a certain area, understanding that although its action may be expensive over the long-term, it nonetheless meets a stated goal. An example would be increasing student financial aid to develop a more diverse student body.

   ♦ The institution may present its expenses using functional categories (for example, instruction, research, libraries, academic support, and so forth) in its financial reports. However, when analyzing the budget, it helps to categorize expenses in their natural categories (for example, salary, benefits, utilities, and so forth). Using the former method, board members can analyze the full cost of program activities, while using the latter allows them to analyze such inflationary factors as salary increases and fringe benefits.[2] Exhibit D displays the statement of functional expenses for SanJo University for 2007 and 2006.

Other key questions related to institutional revenues and expenses include the following:

♦ Are revenues increasing at a faster rate than expenses?

♦ Are expenses increasing in line with or more rapidly than inflation? (Recall that the Higher Education Price Index has generally been higher than the Consumer Price Index since 1976.)[3]

*Analysis.* At 43.9 percent, instruction and research is the university's largest expense, which reflects its priority among the university's activities. At 15.5 percent, general administration (institutional support) is the second largest expense. SanJo University may want to assess more carefully—and possibly reduce—its spending on institutional support if it cannot justify

---

2  While institutions may choose the format for reporting their expenses on the statement of activities, SFAS No. 117 requires all organizations to provide functional expense classifications, whether in a separate statement or in the notes. Some institutions present expenses using both classification systems, because they believe this provides readers with all the necessary information to understand the operating results.

3  Commonfund Institute, "HEPI 2006 Update," 3, Table A.

**Exhibit D** SanJo University statement of functional expenses, FY 2007 and FY 2006

**SanJo University**
**Statement of Functional Expenses**

For the years ended June 30, 2007 and 2006 (in thousands)

| | Instruction and research | Libraries | Academic support | Student services | General admin | Auxiliary enterprises | Total expenses |
|---|---|---|---|---|---|---|---|
| **2007** | | | | | | | |
| Salaries and benefits | $25,202 | $2,993 | $5,339 | $5,103 | $8,930 | $8,403 | $55,969 |
| Purchased services | 3,150 | 374 | 667 | 638 | 1,116 | 1,050 | 6,996 |
| Supplies and general | 1,112 | 132 | 236 | 225 | 394 | 371 | 2,469 |
| Utilities | 1,853 | 220 | 393 | 375 | 657 | 618 | 4,115 |
| Travel | 741 | 88 | 157 | 150 | 263 | 247 | 1,646 |
| Other expenses | 465 | 55 | 99 | 94 | 165 | 155 | 1,033 |
| Depreciation | 3,152 | 374 | 668 | 638 | 1,117 | 1,051 | 7,001 |
| Interest | 1,386 | 165 | 294 | 281 | 491 | 462 | 3,078 |
| | $37,062 | $4,401 | $7,852 | $7,504 | $13,132 | $12,357 | $82,308 |
| **2006** | | | | | | | |
| Salaries and benefits | $24,367 | $2,700 | $5,126 | $4,899 | $8,572 | $8,067 | $53,730 |
| Purchased services | 3,196 | 379 | 677 | 647 | 1,132 | 1,065 | 7,097 |
| Supplies and general | 1,048 | 124 | 222 | 212 | 371 | 349 | 2,326 |
| Utilities | 1,746 | 207 | 370 | 353 | 619 | 582 | 3,877 |
| Travel | 698 | 83 | 148 | 141 | 247 | 233 | 1,551 |
| Other expenses | 438 | 52 | 93 | 89 | 155 | 146 | 973 |
| Depreciation | 2,359 | 280 | 500 | 478 | 836 | 787 | 5,240 |
| Interest | 1,238 | 147 | 263 | 251 | 439 | 413 | 2,749 |
| | $35,090 | $3,972 | $7,398 | $7,070 | $12,372 | $11,642 | $77,544 |

*Because of rounding, totals are not exact.

**Table 5.4** SanJo University 2007 operating expenses

| Operating expenses | 2007 Totals | % of Total revenue |
|---|---|---|
| Instruction and research | $37,062 | 43.9 |
| Libraries | 4,401 | 5.2 |
| Academic support | 7,852 | 9.3 |
| Student services | 7,504 | 8.9 |
| General administration | 13,132 | 15.5 |
| Auxiliaries enterprises | 12,357 | 14.6 |
| Total operating expenses | $82,308 | 97.2 |

the costs with its strategic objectives.

5. **How dependent was the institution on investment or endowment income and annual giving to meet its operating needs?** This question focuses on two increasingly important revenue sources for many colleges and universities: endowment income and fundraising.

*Indicator.* Private gifts and grants, and investment income as a percentage of total operating revenues.

*Factors to consider*

• Most institutions rely on external financial support to meet their operating budgets. It is important to understand the extent to which the institution depends on these revenue sources and whether they are sustainable.

♦ Private giving and investment (endowment) income also increase an institution's operating flexibility, enabling it to leverage other revenue sources, especially tuition. Many colleges and universities are becoming increasingly dependent on this revenue stream.

*Analysis.* In 2007, gifts and investment income provided 24.7 percent of the university's unrestricted operating revenues, which means the university depends on giving and investment spending (portion of the total investment income available for current use) for almost one quarter of its operating revenue. This is significant, making the university dependent on successful fundraising and long-term investment management.

**Table 5.5** Dependency on gifts and investment income

| Revenue source | 2007 Totals | |
| --- | --- | --- |
| | Unrestricted | Temporarily restricted |
| Private gifts and grants | $5,436 | $3,672 |
| Investment income used for operations | 13,594 | 0 |
| | 19,030 | 3,672 |
| Temporarily restricted amounts released for operations | 1,908 | (1,908) |
| Total gifts and investment income used for operations | $20,938 | |
| Total unrestricted operating revenues | $84,689 | |
| Percentage of unrestricted operating revenue | 24.7% | |

6. **Do the auxiliary enterprises of the institution support their own costs?** Auxiliary enterprises traditionally include food services, housing, college stores, and other services. Ideally, they are self-supporting operations.

*Indicator.* The net of auxiliary revenues and auxiliary expenses.

*Factors to consider*

♦ Most colleges and universities provide auxiliary services, which must be priced and operated so they do not financially drain the institution. Most institu-

tions try to operate their auxiliaries near the break-even point on a fully costed basis (that is, the direct and indirect costs are recovered through fees).

♦ It is important to understand the operating results from auxiliary enterprises and the manner in which they are determined. Board members should know if indirect costs—management and administrative costs, the cost of debt service related to the facilities, and noncash costs like depreciation—are used to calculate the operating results for an auxiliary enterprise.

♦ Outsourcing is another consideration. Many institutions are choosing to outsource rather than self-manage certain areas of their operations, especially those unrelated to the institution's mission. Other likely outsourced areas are those in which the institution is not able to break even. An external vendor who specializes in the area (such as bookstores or food services) may be able to operate it more profitably and improve quality as well.

*Analysis.* Table 5.6 indicates the university had net auxiliary services revenue (an operating surplus) of $2,450. This surplus enabled the university to augment certain programs supporting its mission. However, we do not know from the financial statements whether the university fully allocates the actual costs of operating its auxiliary services to the reported line item. Board members should ask about this issue when analyzing the institution's financial condition.

7. **How well did the institution manage its investments?** An important function of the governing board is to ensure that endowments and other invested funds are producing returns consistent with their spending needs and long-term growth objectives. The board, of course, should regularly monitor investment returns. In fact most institu-

**Table 5.6** Auxiliary enterprises

|  | 2007 Totals |
|---|---|
| Sales and services of auxiliaries | $14,807 |
| Auxiliaries expenses | $12,357 |
| Net auxiliary services revenue | $2,450 |

tions with substantial portfolios have board-established investment committees to oversee investing activities.

In 1995 the FASB released "Accounting for Certain Investments Held by Not-for-Profit Organizations" (SFAS No. 124), which specifies the investment data required on not-for-profit statements of activities and accompanying notes. Consequently, most institutions provide sufficient information in their financial statements to analyze its investment performance.

*Indicator.* Total investment return plus net realized and unrealized investment gains minus related management and custodial expenses as a percentage of average market value of the invested assets.

*Factors to consider*

+ Board members must look at total return on investments, which includes interest income and dividends as well as net realized and unrealized gains. Investment return is a function of the types of investments held and the degree of risk the institution is willing to accept.

+ Most institutions have adopted a formal spending policy that permits the use of the yield (dividends and interest) as well as a prudent portion of the portfolio gains for operations.

+ An imbalance among the rates of investment income, spending, and reinvestment can reduce the future purchasing power of the institution's portfolio. Growth must be greater than inflation and use.

*Analysis.* Table 5.7 shows the university's total return was a disappointing 4.2 percent, which raises questions about the university's management of its investments. Note 4 of the financial statements provides details. (See Appendix B.)

**Table 5.7** Investment performance

|  |  | 2007 |
|---|---|---|
| Investment income |  |  |
| Dividends and interest income |  | $9,059 |
| Realized gains (losses) on investments |  | (12,307) |
| Unrealized gains on investments |  | 18,347 |
| Total return* | B | $15,099 |
| Beginnning market value of investments* |  | $301,961 |
| Ending market value of investments* |  | $416,466 |
| Average market value of investments | C | $359,214 |
| Total return on investments | B/C | 4.20% |

*From Appendix B, Note 4.

8. **How well did the institution manage its fundraising?** The statement of activities measures contributions on the accrual basis, which should help readers assess an institution's overall fundraising activities for the year. However, because the various formats report gifts in different places in the statement of activities, the level of charitable giving is not always readily apparent. Some institutions summarize fundraising data in the notes to the financial statements to simplify and enhance the reader's understanding.

In "Accounting for Contributions Received and Contributions Made" (SFAS No. 116), the FASB explains its requirements for reporting charitable giving. Most notable is that colleges and universities should record unconditional pledges: (1) as contributions when the donor makes the commitment and (2) at the present value of the amounts the institution expects to receive. As a result, "gifts" and "contributions" appearing on the statement of activities generally do not equal the cash the institution actually receives from donors during the period. (The statement of cash flows clarifies the level of cash contributions the institution actually receives during the year.) The FASB also requires institutions to disclose the cost of fundraising, either in the statement of activities or in the notes to the financial statements.

The FASB practices for reporting fundraising results are more restrictive than those used by development or advancement offices at most institutions. It is common to see different results in development office reports and the institution's financial statements. The most common differences relate to conditional gifts or bequests, which are not recognized for accounting purposes until they become unconditional gifts, yet may be recognized in development office data.

*Indicator.* Fundraising costs as a percentage of gifts recorded.

*Factors to consider*

+ It is important to understand why giving fluctuates from year to year. Annual giving usually increases as the number and percentage of alumni giving increases. Capital giving generally fluctuates, especially if the institution is in the midst of a capital campaign.

+ Charitable giving decreases an institution's reliance on tuition and other revenue sources as well as its need for external financing for capital projects.

+ An institution may want to compare its charitable-giving trends to those of peer institutions. Bond rating agencies often consider the percentage of alumni (and sometimes the average gift per alumnus) who give to their alma mater as an indicator of their satisfaction with the institution.

+ Development frequently is perceived as an expensive department, which explains why fundraising costs as a percentage of gifts recorded is an important indicator. Although it is not available in the SanJo case study, another important indicator is a summary of annual and capital campaign activity by source (that is, from alumni, other individuals, foundations, corporations, and other sources).

*Analysis.* The fundraising costs in Table 5.8 come from Note 2, "Pledges receivable," in Appendix B. The

data show calculations for different fundraising costs. The university's cost to raise each dollar is about 15 cents for regular fundraising. Because the university is in the middle of a significant capital campaign, it has chosen to segregate the incremental costs of the campaign from the regular fundraising costs.

**Table 5.8** Fundraising efficiency

|                               | **2007** | **2006** |
|-------------------------------|----------|----------|
| Private gifts and grants      | 9,108    | 8,279    |
| Capital gifts                 | 67,291   | 159,411  |
| Total fundraising             | $76,399  | $167,690 |
|                               |          |          |
| Cost of fundraising*          |          |          |
|                               |          |          |
| Regular fundraising costs     | 1,363    | 1,333    |
| Capital campaign costs        | 6,256    | 2,612    |
| Total fundraising costs       | $7,619   | $3,945   |
|                               |          |          |
| Regular fundraising efficiency| 15%      | 16%      |
| Capital fundraising efficiency| 9%       | 2%       |
| Overall fundraising efficiency| 10%      | 2%       |

*From Appendix B, Note 2.

# Summary

The foregoing is a discussion of the most basic questions answered by the statement of activities and its related notes. Board members should also consider issues unique to an institution's operations. In Chapter 7 we return to the statement of activities and use ratios to measure how well the college or university managed its resources.

## *Statement of Activities: Commonly Used Formats*

**Simple nonsegregated format.** This format summarizes the relevant changes within each of the net asset groups without distinguishing between operating and nonoperating activity of the unrestricted net assets. (See Table 5.9.) It is difficult to find important information about fundraising and investment performance, because many of the information categories are repeated within each of the net

**Table 5.9** Statement of activities: Simple nonsegregated format

**SanJo University**
**Statement of Activities**

For the year ended June 30, 2007 (in thousands)

| | Unrestricted | Temporarily restricted | Permanently restricted | Totals |
|---|---|---|---|---|
| **Revenues** | | | | |
| Tuition and fees | $66,300 | | | $66,300 |
| University-sponsored financial aid | (10,294) | | | (10,294) |
| Donor-sponsored financial aid | (11,562) | | | (11,562) |
| Net tuition and fees | 44,444 | | | 44,444 |
| Sales and services of auxiliaries | 14,807 | | | 14,807 |
| Government grants and contracts | 2,750 | | | 2,750 |
| Private gifts and grants | 5,436 | 3,672 | | 9,108 |
| Capital gifts | 2,000 | 10,000 | 55,291 | 67,291 |
| Total investment income | 8,207 | 6,892 | | 15,099 |
| Other | 3,950 | | | 3,950 |
| Net assets released from restrictions | 16,500 | (16,500) | | |
| Total operating revenues | $98,094 | $4,064 | $55,291 | $157,449 |
| | | | | |
| **Expenses** | | | | |
| Instruction and research | 37,062 | | | 37,062 |
| Libraries | 4,401 | | | 4,401 |
| Academic support | 7,852 | | | 7,852 |
| Student services | 7,504 | | | 7,504 |
| General administration | 13,132 | | | 13,132 |
| Auxiliaries enterprises | 12,357 | | | 12,357 |
| Total operating expenses | $82,308 | | | $82,308 |
| | | | | |
| Net increase in net assets | 15,786 | 4,064 | 55,291 | 75,141 |
| Net assets at beginning of year | 183,414 | 99,912 | 329,173 | 612,499 |
| Net assets at end of year | $199,200 | $103,976 | $384,464 | $687,640 |

asset categories. This format also makes it difficult to determine how well the institution is performing except on a highly aggregated basis. In short, it may raise more questions than it answers. Few institutions use this format.

**Stacked operating measure format.** This format segregates activities within the unrestricted net assets. (See Table 5.10.) It clearly displays a measure of operations, "Increases in net assets from operating activities." The reader can see readily which of the

unrestricted net assets changes—for example, contributions and investing activities—the institution considers non-operating. It is still difficult to find important information about fundraising and investment performance, because the information is spread among the three net asset categories.

**Columnar operating measure format.** This format is among the most popular used by colleges and universities. (See Table 5.11.) It not only distinguishes between the operating and non-operating activity of the unrestricted net assets, but it also simplifies and consolidates information about fundraising, investment performance, and the degree to which the institution reinvests or uses such income. SanJo University's statement of activities follows this format.

**Table 5.10** Statement of activities: Stacked operating measure format

**SanJo University**
**Statement of Activities**

For the year ended June 30, 2007 (in thousands)

**Unrestricted operating revenues**

| | |
|---|---:|
| Tuition and fees | $66,300 |
| University-sponsored financial aid | (10,294) |
| Donor-sponsored financial aid | (11,562) |
| Net tuition and fees | 44,444 |
| Sales and services of auxiliaries | 14,807 |
| Government grants and contracts | 2,750 |
| Private gifts and grants | 5,436 |
| Investment income used for operations | 9,002 |
| Other income | 1,750 |
| Net assets released from restrictions | 6,500 |
| Total operating revenues | $84,689 |

**Operating expenses**

| | |
|---|---:|
| Instruction and research | 37,062 |
| Libraries | 4,401 |
| Academic support | 7,852 |
| Student services | 7,504 |
| General administration | 13,132 |
| Auxiliaries enterprises | 12,357 |
| Total operating expenses | $82,308 |
| Increase in net assets from operating activities | $2,381 |

**Nonoperating activities**

| | |
|---|---:|
| Total investment income | 8,207 |
| Less investment income used for operations | (9,002) |
| Capital gifts | 2,000 |
| Other | 2,200 |
| Net assets released from restrictions | 10,000 |
| Net increase in unrestricted net assets | $15,786 |

**Increase in temporarily restricted net assets**

| | |
|---|---:|
| Private gifts and grants | 3,672 |
| Total investment income | 6,892 |
| Capital gifts | 10,000 |
| Net assets released from restrictions | (16,500) |
| Net increase in temporarily restricted net assets | $4,064 |

**Increase in permanently restricted net assets**

| | |
|---|---:|
| Capital gifts | 55,291 |
| Net increase in permanently restricted net assets | $55,291 |
| | |
| Net increase in net assets | 75,141 |
| Net assets at beginning of year | 612,499 |
| Net assets at end of year | $687,640 |

**Table 5.11** Statement of activities: Columnar operating measure format

**SanJo University**
**Statement of Activities**

For the year ended June 30, 2007 (in thousands)

| | Unrestricted | Temporarily restricted | Permanently restriced | 2007 Totals |
|---|---|---|---|---|
| **Operating revenues** | | | | |
| Tuition and fees | $66,300 | | | $66,300 |
| University-sponsored financial aid | (10,294) | | | (10,294) |
| Donor-sponsored financial aid | (11,562) | | | (11,562) |
| Net tuition and fees | 44,444 | | | 44,444 |
| Sales and services of auxiliaries | 14,807 | | | 14,807 |
| Government grants and contracts | 2,750 | | | 2,750 |
| Private gifts and grants | 5,436 | 3,672 | | 9,108 |
| Investment income used for operations | 9,002 | 4,592 | | 13,594 |
| Other income | 1,750 | | | 1,750 |
| Net assets released from restrictions | 6,500 | (6,500) | | |
| Total operating revenues | $84,689 | $1,764 | | $86,453 |
| **Operating expenses** | | | | |
| Instruction and research | 37,062 | | | 37,062 |
| Libraries | 4,401 | | | 4,401 |
| Academic support | 7,852 | | | 7,852 |
| Student services | 7,504 | | | 7,504 |
| General administration | 13,132 | | | 13,132 |
| Auxiliaries enterprises | 12,357 | | | 12,357 |
| Total operating expenses | $82,308 | | | $82,308 |
| Increase in net assets from operating activities | $2,381 | $1,764 | | $4,145 |
| **Nonoperating activities** | | | | |
| Total investment income | 8,207 | 6,892 | | 15,099 |
| Less investment income used for operations | (9,002) | (4,592) | | (13,594) |
| Capital gifts | 2,000 | 10,000 | 55,291 | 67,291 |
| Other | 2,200 | | | 2,200 |
| Net assets released from restrictions | 10,000 | (10,000) | | |
| Increase in net assets from nonoperating activities | $13,405 | $2,300 | $55,291 | $70,996 |
| Net increase in net assets | 15,786 | 4,064 | 55,291 | 75,141 |
| Net assets at beginning of year | 183,414 | 99,912 | 329,173 | 612,499 |
| Net assets at end of year | $199,200 | $103,976 | $384,464 | $687,640 |

# Statement of Cash Flows

The statement of cash flows provides information about the changes in an institution's cash and cash equivalents during a specific period.[1] In "Statement of Cash Flows" (SFAS No. 95), the FASB outlines reporting requirements for not-for-profits, which are similar to those for commercial enterprises.[2] The cash flow statement must present separately cash flows from (1) operating activities, (2) investing activities, and (3) financing activities.

## Operating Activities

The calculation for cash flows from operations begins with the total change in net assets for the period, found on the statement of activities. This amount is then adjusted up or down as follows:

+ Items that did not consume cash—for example, amortization and depreciation—must be added back to total change in net assets.

+ Items that did not provide cash—such as gifts in kind and pledges—are deducted from the total change in net assets.

[1] Cash equivalents are highly liquid investments, which the institution can quickly convert to cash with little risk of value fluctuation caused by interest rates.

[2] Both for-profits and not-for-profits can choose to report their cash flows using either the direct or indirect method. With the direct method, each revenue and expense appears as a separate line item that reflects the cash amounts generated or used by operations. Although it is informative, few independent colleges and universities have adopted this format, because it is difficult to prepare. Interestingly, the Governmental Accounting Standards Board—which oversees accounting standards for public entities, such as public colleges and universities—requires its subjects to use the direct method. The indirect method reconciles the changes in net assets for the institution as a whole, with the amount reflected as the cash flow generated or used by operations. SanJo University uses this method in its statement of cash flows. (See Exhibit C.)

+ Capital and long-term contributions that increase net assets—whether in the form of funds for the acquisition or construction of property, plant, or equipment or new funds for endowment—must also be removed from the total change in net assets. (They should be reclassified with either investing and/or financing activities.)

Finally, items that change an institution's working capital (that is, its current assets and liabilities) also affect cash flows from operations. If accounts receivable increases, the cash flow from the institution's working capital decreases. Conversely, if accounts receivable decreases, the working capital cash flow increases.

## Investing Activities

The second section of the statement of cash flows focuses on investing activities. For the typical college or university, investing activities often include purchase or sales of plant, equipment, and investments.

## Financing Activities

The third section of the statement of cash flows focuses on financing activities. Typical financing activities include the issuance or repayment of long-term debt. Recall that contributions for long-term investment are removed from the institution's operating activities, yet they do provide cash flow. They appear in this section of the statement of cash flows, as they are considered a financing activity.

**Exhibit C** SanJo University statement of cash flows, FY 2007 and FY 2006

**SanJo University**
**Statement of Cash Flows**

For the two years ended June 30, 2007 and 2006 (in thousands)

| | 2007 | 2006 |
|---|---|---|
| **Cash flows from operating activities** | | |
| Change in net assets | $75,141 | $152,908 |
| Adjustments to reconcile change in net assets | | |
| to net cash provided by operating activities: | | |
| Depreciation | 7,001 | 5,240 |
| (Gains) losses on investments | (6,040) | 252 |
| Capital gifts | (105,000) | (65,000) |
| Changes in assets and liabilities that provide (use) cash: | | |
| Accounts receivable | (50) | (130) |
| Short-term investments | (75) | (330) |
| Inventories | (55) | (68) |
| Prepaid expenses and other assets | (93) | (238) |
| Pledges receivable | 42,661 | (96,075) |
| Student loans receivable | (539) | (469) |
| Accounts payable and accrued expenses | 1,177 | 1,012 |
| Deposits and deferred revenues | 727 | 614 |
| Postretirement benefits | 1,251 | 1,089 |
| Other changes | 562 | 489 |
| Net cash provided by (used for) operating activities | $16,668 | ($706) |
| **Cash flows from investing activities** | | |
| Purchases of plant and equipment, net | (25,000) | (50,000) |
| Purchases of investments | (321,624) | (265,814) |
| Proceeds from sales and maturities of investments | 213,159 | 228,131 |
| Net cash used in investing activities | ($133,465) | ($87,683) |
| **Cash flows from financing activities** | | |
| Proceeds from contributions for: | | |
| Investment in endowment | 95,000 | 40,000 |
| Investment in long-lived assets | 10,000 | 25,000 |
| Proceeds from issuance of long-term debt | 15,000 | 25,000 |
| Payments on long-term debt | (3,228) | (1,886) |
| Net cash provided by financing activities | $116,772 | $88,114 |
| Net decrease in cash and cash equivalents | (25) | (275) |
| Cash and cash equivalents, beginning of year | 14,225 | 14,500 |
| Cash and cash equivalents, end of year | $14,200 | $14,225 |
| **Supplemental data** | | |
| Interest paid | $3,078 | $2,749 |

Ultimately, the sum of changes in cash flows from operating, investing, and financing activities equals the total cash and cash equivalents reported in the statement of financial position.

**Table 6.1** Factors affecting cash flows by category

| Cash flows category | Total | Factors affecting cash flows |
|---|---|---|
| Net cash provided by operating activities | $16,668 | The result of collecting pledges receivable (the largest change after removing reconciling items) |
| Net cash used in investing activities | ($133,465) | The result of puchasing more investments and property, net of related investment sales or asset disposals |
| Net cash provided by financing activities | $116,772 | The result of contributions for endowment and long-lived assets as well as net new debt |

## Reading the Statement of Cash Flows for SanJo University

Exhibit C presents the statement of cash flows for SanJo University for FY 2007 and, for comparison, FY 2006. The three major categories—operating activities, investing activities, and financing activities—are indicated in bold. "Supplemental data," which is required by the financial reporting standards, appears at the bottom of the statement.

The statement of cash flows begins with the change in net assets of $75,141, which comes from "Net increase in net assets" from the statement of activities. (See Exhibit B.) After applying the appropriate adjustments, the "Net cash provided by operating activities" for FY 2007 is $16,668.

"Net cash used in investing activities" is $133,465. Because SanJo invested contributions received for new endowment funds, it used more cash than it earned for investing activities in FY 2007. "Net cash provided by financing activities" is $116,772, largely the result of contributions received for long-term investment and new borrowings.

The net result of changes in the three categories is a $25 "Net decrease in cash and cash equivalents," resulting in a year-end balance of $14,200. This figure appears as the final line on the statement of cash flows and as the first asset listed on the statement of financial position. (See Exhibit C and Exhibit A, respectively.)

## Analyzing the Statement of Cash Flows

The statement of cash flows answers the strategic question: *What are the institution's sources of cash, and how has it used them for operating, investing, and financing activities?* Table 6.1 lists actions that influenced each area of activity.

## Summary

The cash flow statement helps readers determine how a college or university finances plant expansion, how it reinvests in its future, and whether there is operating cash available for important commitments such as deferred-maintenance programs and debt service. More specific questions might include:

- Is the overall net change in cash positive?

- Are operating cash flows positive? Does the institution have to rely on other sources of cash to meet operating needs?

- What are the sources of cash to finance either renovation or new construction of facilities?

- Is the college or university generating cash to meet debt services (that is, repayment of principal and interest)?

While this chapter has provided a basic understanding of the statement of cash flows, Chapter 7 introduces several ratios to assess liquidity, which measures an institution's ability to meet current operating costs.

# CHAPTER 7

# External Markets and Ratio Analysis

In Chapter 2, we introduced the primary user groups of financial statements: resource providers, constituents, governing and oversight bodies, and internal users. In this chapter, we examine how these groups—or stakeholders—use financial statements to make decisions about a college or university. In particular, we discuss several ratios that indicate an institution's financial condition.

Most college and university stakeholders include donors, sponsors, lenders, investors, regulators, parents, students, faculty, staff, and peers. Of particular importance are rating agencies, such as Moody's Investors Service, Fitch Ratings, and Standard and Poor's. They view higher education as a business, so they analyze college and university financial statements in much the same way they would a for-profit entity. To establish credit ratings, they focus on key questions such as:

+ *Market position.* What are the trends in applications, acceptances, and deposits broken down by undergraduate and graduate programs? Who are the top competitors (benchmark institutions)?

+ *Financial performance.* Is the institution financially sound and sustainable? What are the trends in revenues, expenses, annual giving, capital campaigns, and endowment returns?

+ *Debt position.* Is debt used appropriately as part of the capital structure?

+ *Legal structure.* How is the debt of the organization secured?

+ *Management.* Does the management team have the expertise to run an effective organization? What is the composition of the board? Does the institution have an attainable strategic plan?

Information from the financial statements, comparative financial ratios, and 5-to-10-year trends helps to answer these questions. However, remember that external factors—such as governmental, economic, and demographic influences—also affect an institution's financial health.

Rating agencies also use nonfinancial information to assess the credit worthiness of an institution. Some factors are:

+ Admissions flexibility

+ Geographic diversity of the student body

+ Student demand

+ Quality, number, and tenure status of the faculty

+ Program offerings

+ Competitive position

+ Management strategies

Although they are nonfinancial, these factors affect an institution's financial statements. For example, rating agencies view student demand as a strong indicator of an institution's long-term financial viability. These factors provide qualitative information that add meaning to the numbers. Accordingly, some rating agencies, like Moody's and S&P, meet with institutional managers to better understand their strategy.

In addition to the financial markets, the federal government has heightened its scrutiny of institutions that receive federal funding for research and student financial aid programs. Not only must financial statements show that the institution can meet debt obligations, that the available reserves can support current operations, and that the institution can live within its means, but programs must comply with federal regulations as well.

Board members must be aware of how stakeholders use financial statements to judge an institution's financial health. External assessments are critical when colleges and universities seek additional funds, such as debt financing, foundation funding, or capital campaign fundraising. It is equally important for boards to do a self-assessment of the institution's financial health.

One tool for assessment is using comparative ratios. In this chapter, we look at how ratios and trends measure an institution's management of its operating results, cash flows, liquidity, and financial viability. We use SanJo University's financial statements to illustrate three groups of financial ratios: (1) operating, (2) financial strength, and (3) cash flow.

## Operating Ratios

Operating ratios help determine whether an institution is living within its means. The information for

these ratios comes primarily from the statement of activities, so they answer the same strategic question as the statement of activities: *How did the institution use its resources to provide service to its constituents?* Combined with trend information, operating ratios also indicate possibly significant changes in the relationship between revenues and expenses.

We cover the following operating ratios:

| | |
|---|---|
| · Operating revenue | · Expendable net assets |
| · Tuition discount | · Debt service |
| · Net operating income | |

Within each group of ratios—operating, financial strength, and cash flow—there are key ratios that all institutions should review regularly. For operating ratios, those ratios are operating revenue and expendable net assets. Debt service is important for institutions that have debt, and tuition discount is important for tuition-dependent institutions.

**Operating revenue.** This ratio captures the institution's dependency on its operating revenue to meet its operating expenses. The ratio is the operating revenue divided by the educational and general expenses.

**Ratio 1** Operating revenue ratio measures dependency on operating revenue to meet operating expenses.

**Operating revenue ratio =**

| | | 2003 | 2004 | 2005 | 2006 | 2007 |
|---|---|---|---|---|---|---|
| **Operating revenue** | **A** | 75.38% | 78.54% | 77.98% | 74.84% | 73.47% |
| **Educational and general expense** | **B** | | | | | |
| | | | | | | |
| **Operating revenue** | | | | | | |
| Net tuition | | 35,739 | 39,165 | 40,852 | 42,638 | 44,444 |
| Auxiliary enterprise revenue | | 10,628 | 12,099 | 13,430 | 14,101 | 14,807 |
| Less: Auxiliary enterprise expenses | | (8,845) | (10,020) | (10,716) | (11,642) | (12,357) |
| Unrestricted grants and contracts | | 1,684 | 1,991 | 2,289 | 2,633 | 2,750 |
| Other unrestricted income[a] | | 1,285 | 1,314 | 1,445 | 1,590 | 1,750 |
| | **A** | $40,491 | $44,549 | $47,300 | $49,320 | $51,394 |
| | | | | | | |
| **Educational and general expense** | | | | | | |
| All operating expenses | | 62,563 | 66,740 | 71,373 | 77,544 | 82,308 |
| Auxiliary operating expenses (netted above) | | (8,845) | (10,020) | (10,716) | (11,642) | (12,357) |
| | **B** | $53,718 | $56,720 | $60,657 | $65,902 | $69,951 |

[a]   Excludes long-term investment income, gains used for operations, and contributions.

**Ratio 2** Tuition discount ratios measure (1) the percentage of financial aid that is donor-supported, and (2) the portion that is effectively an institutional discount to achieve enrollment objectives.

**Tuition discount ratios:**

| | | 2003 | 2004 | 2005 | 2006 | 2007 |
|---|---|---|---|---|---|---|
| Total financial aid[a] | **B** | | | | | |
| Tuition and fees | **C** | 30.34% | 27.47% | 31.73% | 32.30% | 32.97% |
| | | | | | | |
| Non-donor-supported financial aid[b] | **A** | | | | | |
| Tuition and fees | **C** | 13.00% | 8.98% | 14.18% | 14.84% | 15.53% |
| | | | | | | |
| University-sponsored financial aid | **A** | 6,671 | 4,849 | 8,484 | 9,347 | 10,294 |
| Donor-sponsored financial aid | | 8,892 | 9,988 | 10,500 | 11,000 | 11,562 |
| Total financial aid | **B** | 15,563 | 14,837 | 18,984 | 20,347 | 21,856 |
| Tuition and fees | **C** | $51,302 | $54,002 | $59,836 | $62,985 | $66,300 |

[a] Total financial aid includes all aid from all sources provided by the institution.

[b] Non-donor-supported financial aid includes all aid provided by the institution from its operating budget other than donor funds and true endowment income for scholarships.

From 2003 to 2007, SanJo's operating revenue ratio ranged from 73 percent to nearly 79 percent, indicating the university depends on its operating revenues to support its educational and general expenses. However, SanJo appears to be lessening its dependence on operating revenues, as the ratio has decreased over the last three years.

**Tuition discount.** Tuition discounting is a critical issue facing colleges and universities. To be competitive, colleges and universities have increased financial aid budgets—in some cases, without considering the long-term implications. If financial aid budgets increase faster than tuition rates, the institution will face budgetary challenges.

Financial aid becomes especially important when it is unfunded because it functions as a tuition discount. When endowment income and aid-designated gifts and grants support financial aid, they make up for the lost revenue caused by tuition discounts. The two tuition discount ratios highlight the difference between all institutional financial aid and the portion thereof that is unfunded. Thus, to calculate these ratios, colleges and universities must show tuition revenue net of any institutional aid.[1]

The first ratio indicates the total discounting that occurs through all institutional sources of aid. It is calculated as follows:

$$\frac{\text{Total institutional financial aid}}{\text{Tuition and fees}}$$

The second ratio measures the total nonfunded institutional aid as a percentage of tuition and fees. It is calculated as follows:

$$\frac{\text{Non-donor-supported financial aid}}{\text{Tuition and fees}}$$

This second ratio is a true measure of the institutional discount because it represents the portion of lost tuition and fees that is not matched by other sources of revenue.[2]

Over the past five years, SanJo University's total institutional aid ranged from 27 percent to nearly 33 percent of tuition and fees, which is similar to that of many institutions. While total aid in 2007 is 33 percent, only half of that amount is unfunded (that is, a "true" discount of tuition and fees). The university has grown the funded portion of financial aid over the five-year period, a positive result of fundraising specif-

[1] The American Institute of Certified Public Accountants (AICPA) requires colleges and universities to disclose tuition revenue, net of any institutional aid in "Not-for-Profit Organizations—AICPA Audit and Accounting Guide."

[2] SanJo's statement of activities itemizes university-sponsored financial aid, but this presentation is not required. Many financial statements show "financial aid" without indicating how much is funded and unfunded.

**Ratio 3** Net operating income ratios measure return on revenues (sales).

**Net operating income ratios:**

| | | 2003 | 2004 | 2005 | 2006 | 2007 |
|---|---|---|---|---|---|---|
| **(Net operating surplus or deficit) - (Investment income + Contributions)**[a] / **Total operating revenue** | A / C | -20.75% | -17.33% | -17.98% | -20.77% | -21.91% |
| **Net operating income or deficit**[b] / **Total operating revenue** | B / C | 1.87% | 4.96% | 3.93% | 2.85% | 2.81% |
| Increase in unrestricted net assets from operations | B | 1,194 | 3,480 | 2,918 | 2,275 | 2,381 |
| Less: Investment income used for operations | | (5,551) | (5,301) | (7,465) | (8,193) | (9,002) |
| Unrestricted private gifts and grants | | (3,980) | (4,084) | (4,492) | (4,941) | (5,436) |
| Temporarily restricted net assets released from restrictions | | (4,890) | (6,266) | (4,318) | (5,723) | (6,500) |
| | A | (13,227) | (12,171) | (13,357) | (16,582) | (18,557) |
| Operating revenue | C | $63,757 | $70,220 | $74,291 | $79,819 | $84,689 |

[a] This ratio includes net operating income from only exchange-type transactions divided by all operating revenues.
[b] This ratio includes net operating income from all sources divided by all operating revenues.

ically for student financial aid. University-sponsored financial aid has increased 54 percent over the five years, while tuition and fees have increased only 29 percent. Therefore, the institution is moving towards increased funding of institutional aid.

**Net operating income.** Net operating income ratios measure the surplus (or deficit) resulting from operations, measured both with and without investment income and contributions. The first ratio excludes investment income and contributions, thus looking at the institution's revenues and expenses from exchange-type transactions. It helps answer questions like "Do tuition and fees cover operating expenses?"

$$\frac{\text{(Net operating surplus or deficit)} - \text{(Investment income} + \text{Contributions)}}{\text{Total operating revenue}}$$

The second net operating income ratio includes all income designated as operating income, such as the amounts spent under the institution's "spending policy"[3] and contributions that were available for operating purposes.

Keep in mind that few institutions are capable of meeting all their operating expenses from tuition, fees, and other sales-type revenues. They often budget a spending rate, which is an estimate of investment income and contributions needed to meet operating expenses. If a college or university uses more than the budgeted spending rate and contributions, it could indicate that either tuition revenues failed to meet operating expenses or that expenses exceeded expectations.

Over the past five years, SanJo University's net operating income ratio without investment income and contributions has averaged around a 20 percent deficit with a trend toward a 22 percent deficit. However, with the inclusion of investment income and contributions, the university shows a consistent but small surplus. These results suggest that net tuition and fees cover approximately 64 percent of the real cost to educate students, and the university's investment income and contributions more than make up for the shortfall. The surplus is small, but that may not be of concern if the institution's overall net worth is growing for other reasons.[4]

**Expendable net assets.** Expendable net assets are those net assets that the college or university can use

---

[3] We examine spending policies in the discussion of the total return on long-term investments ratio later in this chapter.

[4] This is the case for SanJo University, as we will discover when calculating the increase in net assets ratio.

for operating expenditures. They typically include unrestricted net assets (other than net investment in plant) and temporarily restricted net assets available to meet future operating expenses.[5]

These ratios, then, measure expendable net assets in relation to operating expenses. The unrestricted expendable net assets ratio is more conservative because it considers only unrestricted net assets that are available for operating purposes:

$$\frac{\text{(Unrestricted net assets)} - \text{(Net investment in plant)}}{\text{Total operating expenses}}$$

The second includes temporarily restricted net assets that may be available to meet future operating costs:

$$\frac{\text{(Expendable net assets)} - \text{(Net investment in plant)}}{\text{Total operating expenses}}$$

A ratio greater than 100 percent indicates an institution has sufficient resources (expendable net assets) to meet one year's expenses and debt repayment even if it earns

no future revenue. Essentially, these ratios measure an institution's financial flexibility if its revenues drop.

For SanJo University, both of these ratios have declined—to 126 percent for the first ratio and to 252 percent for the second—over the past five years, indicating the university's net assets to cover operating expenses has decreased. The ratios also show that despite increases in expendable net assets over the five year period, operating expenses have grown more rapidly. Still, the ratio levels are more than adequate, demonstrating reasonable strength if the university's operating income were to decline.

**Debt service.** These ratios gauge an institution's ability to meet its debt obligations. The calculations incorporate "annual debt service," which is the sum of interest expense (from the statement of activities) and principal repayment (from the statement of cash flows).

The "debt service to operating expenses ratio" measures the effect of debt service on the overall cost of operations.

**Ratio 4** Expendable net assets ratios measure (1) the unrestricted resources available, and (2) all resources available for expenditure against one year's operating costs.

**Expendable net assets ratios:**

| | | 2003 | 2004 | 2005 | 2006 | 2007 |
|---|---|---|---|---|---|---|
| **(Unrestricted net assets) – (Net investment in plant)** | **A** | 161% | 144% | 130% | 121% | 126% |
| **Total operating expenses** | **B** | | | | | |
| Unrestricted net assets | | 147,341 | 157,212 | 160,508 | 183,414 | 199,200 |
| Less: Investment in plant | | (46,491) | (61,047) | (67,875) | (89,521) | (95,748) |
| | **A** | 100,850 | 96,165 | 92,633 | 93,893 | 103,452 |
| Total operating expenses | **B** | $62,563 | $66,740 | $71,373 | $77,544 | $82,308 |
| **(Expendable net assets) – (Net investment in plant)** | **C** | 311% | 299% | 269% | 250% | 252% |
| **Total operating expenses** | **B** | | | | | |
| Unrestricted net assets | | 147,341 | 157,212 | 160,508 | 183,414 | 199,200 |
| Temporarily restricted net assets | | 93,522 | 103,537 | 99,321 | 99,912 | 103,976 |
| Less: Investment in plant | | (46,491) | (61,047) | (67,875) | (89,521) | (95,748) |
| | **C** | $194,372 | $199,702 | $191,954 | $193,805 | $207,428 |

[5]  Net investment in plant includes the institution's investment in property, plant, and equipment minus any related debt.

$$\frac{\text{Annual debt service}}{\text{(Operating expenses)} + \text{(Debt principal repayment)}^*}$$

*Principal repayments include only the normal required amortization of debt. It should not include prepayments or refinancings.

As this percentage increases, an institution must spend more on debt service, which reduces amounts available for other expenses. Also, the higher the percentage, the less financial flexibility an institution has if its operating or economic conditions change. Ideally, colleges and universities should keep their debt service ratio in the 5 percent to 10 percent range. For SanJo, this ratio has been slowly growing to its current value of 7.4 percent.

The "debt service coverage ratio" measures the ability of the institution to meet debt service obligations from operating resources. This ratio calculates the operating surplus and interest expense as a percentage of annual debt service. Results greater than 100 percent indicate a college or university is able to meet its debt obligations from current operating resources.

$$\frac{\text{(Operating surplus)} + \text{(Interest expense)}}{\text{Annual debt service}}$$

The debt service coverage ratio for SanJo University has declined to 87 percent over the past five years, as it has taken on more long-term debt. Because the ratio is below 100 percent, it could be an issue with lenders.

# Financial Strength Ratios

Financial strength ratios measure the solvency, financial flexibility, and long-term viability of a college

**Ratio 5** Debt service ratios measure (1) the percentage of debt service to the total operating costs of the institution, and (2) the ability of the institution to meet debt service obligations from normal operating sources.

**Debt service to operating expenses ratio =**

| | | 2003 | 2004 | 2005 | 2006 | 2007 |
|---|---|---|---|---|---|---|
| $\dfrac{\text{Annual debt service}^a}{\text{(Operating expenses)} + \text{(Debt principal repayment)}}$ | A<br>B | 5.27% | 5.04% | 29.94% | 5.84% | 7.37% |
| Interest expense[b] | | 2,286 | 2,279 | 2,093 | 2,749 | 3,078 |
| Required principal payments on debt[b] | | 1,068 | 1,141 | 27,514 | 1,886 | 3,228 |
| | A | 3,354 | 3,420 | 29,607 | 4,635 | 6,306 |
| Total operating expenses | | 62,563 | 66,740 | 71,373 | 77,544 | 82,308 |
| Debt principal repayment[b] | | 1,068 | 1,141 | 27,514 | 1,886 | 3,228 |
| | B | $63,631 | $67,881 | $98,887 | $79,430 | $85,536 |

**Debt service coverage ratio =**

| | | 2003 | 2004 | 2005 | 2006 | 2007 |
|---|---|---|---|---|---|---|
| $\dfrac{\text{(Operating surplus)} + \text{(Interest expense)}}{\text{Annual debt service}^a}$ | C<br>A | 104% | 168% | 17% | 108% | 87% |
| Increase in unrestricted net assets | | 1,194 | 3,480 | 2,918 | 2,275 | 2,381 |
| Interest expense[b] | | 2,286 | 2,279 | 2,093 | 2,749 | 3,078 |
| Operating surplus plus interest expense | C | $3,480 | $5,759 | $5,011 | $5,024 | $5,459 |

[a]Annual debt service = Interest expense + Principal repayments.
[b]From statement of cash flows or accompanying notes.

**Ratio 6** Endowment per FTE student ratio measures the size of the endowment relative to enrollment.

**Endowment per FTE student ratio =**

| | 2003 | 2004 | 2005 | 2006 | 2007 |
|---|---|---|---|---|---|
| $\dfrac{\text{Total endowment}}{\text{Number of FTE students}}$ | $133,127 | $141,413 | $190,669 | $260,845 | $295,738 |
| Number of full-time equivalent (FTE) students | 1,618 | 1,617 | 1,700 | 1,702 | 1,700 |

or university by focusing on its debt and endowment. Information for financial strength ratios comes primarily from the statement of financial position. Together, the ratios and the statement answer the strategic question: *Are existing resources sufficient to enable the institution to fulfill its mission?* The greater its endowment and the lower its debt, the more flexibility a college or university has in addressing changes in its revenue and expense streams.

Financial strength ratios include:

| | |
|---|---|
| · Endowment per FTE student | · Total debt to expendable net assets |
| · Total debt to expendable unrestricted net assets | · Increase in net assets |
| | · Total return on long-term investments |

The key financial strength ratio is the increase in net assets. The endowment and total return ratios are important for institutions with significant endowments, while the debt ratios are important for institutions that have significant debt or that are contemplating additional borrowings.

**Endowment per FTE student.** The endowment per full-time equivalent (FTE) student ratio measures the size of an institution's endowment relative to its enrollment. The higher the ratio, the more flexibility an institution has to meet rising costs and provide quality programs without increasing tuition. Without endowment—and often a significant one—an institution's only recourse is to increase its tuition and fees.

For SanJo, the endowment per FTE student has risen to $295,738. With 1,700 FTE students, the endowment is relatively high in comparison to similar institutions.

**Total debt to expendable unrestricted net assets.** This ratio measures the ability of an institution to meet its outstanding debt solely from unrestricted net assets.[6]

$$\frac{\text{Total debt outstanding}}{\text{(Unrestricted net assets)} - \text{(Net investment in plant)}}$$

Many institutions find it more beneficial to use tax-exempt offerings to finance projects than to use its unrestricted net assets, which could earn higher returns from other investment opportunities. In general, however, the higher the ratio of debt to expendable unrestricted net assets, the more highly leveraged the institution is, and the less flexibility it has to increase its borrowing. Note that expendable net assets (the denominator for this ratio) excludes plant assets, because they are not liquid. As a result, this is a conservative measure of debt to equity.

SanJo University's total debt outstanding to expendable unrestricted net assets ratio has increased dramatically from 49 to 94 percent in the last five years, as the university has borrowed heavily using tax-exempt debt. Ideally, colleges and universities want to keep this ratio at or below 100 percent, which translates to a 50:50 relationship of long-term debt to unrestricted expendable net assets. SanJo is right at this threshold.

**Total debt to expendable net assets.** This ratio measures the relationship of outstanding debt to all expendable net assets. Like the previous ratio, it includes all unrestricted net assets minus net investment in plant assets. However, it is more informative, as it also includes temporarily restricted net assets

---

6   This ratio is similar to a debt to liquid equity ratio for a corporate enterprise.

**Ratios 7(1) and 7(2)** Total debt to expendable net assets ratios measure the ability of the institution to meet outstanding debt from (1) unrestricted net assets and (2) all net assets which ultimately may be expended.

**1. Total debt to expendable unrestricted net assets ratio =**

| | | 2003 | 2004 | 2005 | 2006 | 2007 |
|---|---|---|---|---|---|---|
| Total debt outstanding | A | | | | | |
| (Unrestricted net assets) – (Net investment in plant) | B | 49.30% | 50.52% | 67.32% | 91.04% | 94.01% |
| | | | | | | |
| Total debt outstanding | A | 49,720 | 48,579 | 62,365 | 85,479 | 97,251 |
| | | | | | | |
| Unrestricted net assets | | 147,341 | 157,212 | 160,508 | 183,414 | 199,200 |
| Less: Net investment in plant | | (46,491) | (61,047) | (67,875) | (89,521) | (95,748) |
| | B | $100,850 | $96,165 | $92,633 | $93,893 | $103,452 |

**2. Total debt to expendable net assets ratio =**

| | | 2003 | 2004 | 2005 | 2006 | 2007 |
|---|---|---|---|---|---|---|
| Total debt outstanding | A | | | | | |
| (Expendable net assets)[a] – (Net investment in plant) | C | 25.58% | 24.33% | 32.49% | 44.11% | 46.88% |
| | | | | | | |
| Unrestricted net assets | | 147,341 | 157,212 | 160,508 | 183,414 | 199,200 |
| Temporarily restricted net assets | | 93,522 | 103,537 | 99,321 | 99,912 | 103,976 |
| Less: Net investment in plant | | (46,491) | (61,047) | (67,875) | (89,521) | (95,748) |
| | C | $194,372 | $199,702 | $191,954 | $193,805 | $207,428 |

[a]  Expendable net assets = Unrestricted + Temporarily restricted net assets.

that will be available to meet the institution's obligations, operating and otherwise. Remember that temporarily restricted net assets become available to the institution as the donor's restrictions are met or with the passage of time, so it is appropriate to consider them as available to the institution.

$$\frac{\text{Total debt outstanding}}{\text{(Expendable net assets)} - \text{(Net investment in plant)}}$$

With the inclusion of the temporarily restricted net assets, SanJo's total debt to expendable net assets ratio from 2003 to 2007 increases from about 26 percent to almost 47 percent, the result of its increased borrowing. Generally, a ratio lower than 50 percent is considered good; below 25 percent is excellent.

These ratios work in concert with the debt coverage ratios. (See Ratio 5.) SanJo's increasing debt to expendable net assets ratios, together with its relatively high debt service ratios, suggest that the university may have difficulty securing additional borrowings, unless it is for facilities that would generate enough additional operating cash flow to cover the new debt service.

**Increase in net assets.** This ratio measures the growth in an institution's total equity. An increase indicates a college or university is adding to its reserves. However, the increase must be greater than inflation if the financial resources are to achieve real growth. The increase in net assets ratio is

$$\frac{\text{Total increase in net assets}}{\text{Total net assets beginning balance}}$$

SanJo University's ratio has fluctuated widely over the past five years with the smallest increase at 7.5 percent and the largest at 34.6 percent. Each year it exceeded the rate of inflation (as measured by the inflation indi-

**Ratio 8** Increase in net assets ratio measures the growth in the institution's equity. This ratio should be compared to an objective measure of inflation to determine if there is real equity growth.

**Increase in net assets ratio =**

| | | 2003 | 2004 | 2005 | 2006 | 2007 |
|---|---|---|---|---|---|---|
| Total increase in net assets | A | 8.40% | 7.51% | 34.61% | 33.27% | 12.27% |
| Total net assets beginning balance | B | | | | | |
| Total increase in net assets | A | 24,610 | 23,850 | 118,178 | 152,908 | 75,141 |
| Net assets at the beginning of the year | B | $292,953 | $317,563 | $341,413 | $459,591 | $612,499 |

ces). In 2005 and 2006, the university was in the midst of its capital campaign, so the ratio reached ten times the rate of inflation.

**Total return on long-term investments.** This ratio measures the total return on an institution's investments, including investment income and the realized and unrealized gains on the investment portfolio.

$$\frac{\text{(Investment income)} + \text{(Realized + Unrealized gains)}}{\text{Average long-term investments for the period}}$$

Most institutions have investment policies that include long-term growth as a major objective for their investments, particularly their endowment funds. At the same time, the college or university must meet its needs for current operating income. Accordingly, boards of trustees have adopted spending rate policies that permit the use of the yield (dividends and interest) as well as a prudent portion of the portfolio gains. In many institutions, this translates to a spending formula of approximately 4 to 6 percent of the portfolio's average fair value. If an institution is to achieve real long-term growth, the total return on long-term investments must exceed both inflation and the spending formula amounts.

The total return on SanJo's long-term investments for the past five years has fluctuated widely ranging from a loss of 4.85 percent to a gain of 10.16 percent, aver-

**Ratio 9** Total return on long-term investments ratio measures the investment performance for the period. This ratio must be measured against the institution's spending policy and inflation to determine if the investments achieved real equity growth.

**Total return on long-term investments ratio =**

| | | 2003 | 2004 | 2005 | 2006 | 2007 |
|---|---|---|---|---|---|---|
| (Investment income) + (Realized + Unrealized gains) | B | 5.23% | 10.16% | -4.85% | 2.71% | 4.20% |
| Average long-term investments for the period | A | | | | | |
| Long-term investments at the beginning of the year | | 237,221 | 240,743 | 249,152 | 264,530 | 301,961 |
| Long-term investments at the end of the year | | 240,743 | 249,152 | 264,530 | 301,961 | 416,466 |
| | | 477,964 | 489,895 | 513,682 | 566,491 | 718,427 |
| Simple average of long-term investments | A | 238,982 | 244,948 | 256,841 | 283,246 | 359,214 |
| Dividends and interest income | | 10,152 | 9,053 | 7,474 | 7,936 | 9,059 |
| Realized and unrealized gains (losses) | | 2,356 | 15,845 | (19,931) | (252) | 6,040 |
| Total investment income | B | $12,508 | $24,898 | $(12,457) | $7,684 | $15,099 |

**Ratio 10** Working capital ratio measures institution's ability to meet working capital requirements in due course.

**Working capital ratio =**

| | | 2003 | 2004 | 2005 | 2006 | 2007 |
|---|---|---|---|---|---|---|
| **Current assets**[a] | **A** | | | | | |
| **Current liabilities**[b] | **B** | 312% | 354% | 294% | 258% | 224% |
| Current assets | | | | | | |
|   Cash and cash equivalents | | 15,650 | 14,866 | 14,500 | 14,225 | 14,200 |
|   Accounts receivable, net | | 851 | 1,010 | 1,520 | 1,650 | 1,700 |
|   Short-term investments | | 11,326 | 11,993 | 10,520 | 10,850 | 10,925 |
|   Inventories | | 1,062 | 1,109 | 1,257 | 1,325 | 1,380 |
|   Prepaid and other assets | | 2,148 | 2,130 | 2,187 | 2,425 | 2,518 |
| | **A** | $31,037 | $31,108 | $29,984 | $30,475 | $30,723 |
| Current liabilities | | | | | | |
|   Accounts payable and accrued expenses | | 7,188 | 5,903 | 6,788 | 7,800 | 8,977 |
|   Deposits and deferred revenues | | 2,759 | 2,897 | 3,419 | 4,033 | 4,760 |
| | **B** | $9,947 | $8,800 | $10,207 | $11,833 | $13,737 |

a  Current assets include all unrestricted amounts expected to be converted to cash in the next 12 months.

b  Current liabilities include all amounts payable or accrued, which are expected to be paid during the next 12 months. (They do not include long-term accruals, such as those for postretirement benefits.)

aging only 3.5 percent for the period. Assuming an average inflation rate of approximately 3 percent for the period, the real return is only about 0.5 percent before endowment spending to support operations. Given the university's 5 percent endowment spending rate (determined by the three-year moving average of the opening fair value of its endowment investments), SanJo has actually experienced a performance deficit of approximately 4.5 percent during the most recent five years as follows:

| | Five-year average (%) |
|---|---|
| Return on investments | 3.50 |
| Rate of inflation | -3.00 |
| Spending rate | -5.00 |
| Overall performance | -4.50 |

Despite the poor investment performance, the university's long-term investments grew from $240 million in 2003 to over $416 million in 2007, a result of donor support from the capital campaign.

# Liquidity and Cash Flow Ratios

Liquidity and cash flow ratios help stakeholders understand an institution's ability to meet current operating costs, investing needs, and financing obligations. The information for these ratios comes from the statement of cash flows, which answers the strategic question: *What are the institution's sources of cash and how has it used them for its operating, investing, and financing activities?*

Liquidity and cash flow ratios include

| | |
|---|---|
| • Working capital | • Capital maintenance funding capability |
| • Operating cash flow to debt service | • Nonliquid net assets |

In this set, working capital is a key ratio for most institutions.

**Working capital.** This ratio measures the ability of an institution to meet its daily working capital requirements by comparing its current assets to current liabilities. Current assets and current liabilities are those that the college or university expects to convert to cash (or to pay liabilities) within one year. The ratio is

$$\frac{\text{Current assets}}{\text{Current liabilities}}$$

SanJo University has a strong working capital ratio, ranging from 312 percent in 2003 to 224 percent in 2007. In other words, at the end of 2007 the university had $2.24 of current assets for each dollar of current liabilities. The downward trend is not alarming, because 224 percent is a strong ratio and perhaps indicative of better cash management. With cash and short-term investments totaling almost $25 million, some may question whether SanJo is too liquid. Perhaps deploying more of its assets with long-term investments could help improve the university's total return on all investments.

**Operating cash flow to debt service.** This ratio measures financial viability, gauging an institution's ability to meet debt service from its operating cash flow. The numerator represents the cash provided by operations and interest expense. The denominator represents an institution's debt service, which is principal and interest. The larger the ratio, the greater the likelihood the institution can meet its debt service requirements from operating income. Ratios below 100 percent indicate an institution needs other sources of financing to meet its current debt.

SanJo University's operating cash flow to debt service ratio was 313 percent at the end of 2007, indicating the university could meet its debt service 3.13 times, based on the cash provided by its operations.

**Annual capital maintenance funding capability.** These ratios measure an institution's ability to fund repairs and replacements of plant assets with cash flows from operations. It should be noted that there is no easy way to determine an institution's capital maintenance needs from its financial statements. In fact, two institutions with almost identical financial statements could—and often do—differ dramatically in this area. Still, it is possible to measure the funds that are available to meet an institution's annual capital maintenance needs. To do that, we use historical cost depreciation and replacement cost depreciation as surrogates for funding capital maintenance. The two ratios are

$$\frac{\text{(Net cash provided by operating activities)} - \text{(Debt service principal)}}{\text{Historical depreciation expense}}$$

$$\frac{\text{(Net cash provided by operating activities)} - \text{(Debt service principal)}}{\text{Replacement cost depreciation expense}}$$

The second ratio is a more conservative measure,

**Ratio 11** Operating cash flow to debt service ratios measures ability of institution to meet debt service from operating cash flows.

**Operating cash flow to debt service ratio =**

| | | 2003 | 2004 | 2005 | 2006 | 2007 |
|---|---|---|---|---|---|---|
| **(Net cash provided by operating activities) + (Interest expense)** | **A** | 432% | 207% | 28% | 44% | 313% |
| **Annual debt service**[a] | **B** | | | | | |
| | | | | | | |
| Net cash provided by operating activities | | 12,206 | 4,784 | 6,157 | (706) | 16,668 |
| Interest expense | | 2,286 | 2,279 | 2,093 | 2,749 | 3,078 |
| | **A** | $14,492 | $7,063 | $8,250 | $2,043 | $19,746 |
| | | | | | | |
| Required principal payments on debt | | 1,068 | 1,141 | 27,514 | 1,886 | 3,228 |
| Interest expense | | 2,286 | 2,279 | 2,093 | 2,749 | 3,078 |
| | **B** | $3,354 | $3,420 | $29,607 | $4,635 | $6,306 |

[a]  Annual debt service = Interest expense + Principal repayments.

**Ratio 12** Annual capital maintenance funding capability ratios measure the ability of the institution to fund its capital maintenance needs. These ratios are approximations at best.

**Annual capital maintenance funding capability ratios:**

|  |  | 2003 | 2004 | 2005 | 2006 | 2007 |
|---|---|---|---|---|---|---|
| **(Net cash provided by operating activities) – (Debt service principal)** | **A** | 333% | 84% | -487% | -49% | 192% |
| **Historical depreciation expense** | **B** | | | | | |
| Net cash provided by operating activities | | 12,206 | 4,784 | 6,157 | (706) | 16,668 |
| Less: Debt service principal[a] | | (1,068) | (1,141) | (27,514) | (1,886) | (3,228) |
| | **A** | $11,138 | $3,643 | $(21,357) | $(2,592) | $13,440 |
| Depreciation expense (from the statement of cash flows or notes) | **B** | 3,342 | 4,334 | 4,386 | 5,240 | 7,001 |

|  |  |  |
|---|---|---|
| **(Net cash provided by operating activities) – (Debt service principal)** | **A** | 69% |
| **Replacement cost depreciation expense*** | **C** | |

\* Replacement cost depreciation is not typically available in basic financial statements. However, many institutions use some method to estimate the expected cost of deferred maintenance. One imperfect method is to determine depreciation using estimated replacement cost, which should be available from insurance records, assuming normal coverage for property damage.

|  | 2007 | | | |
|---|---|---|---|---|
|  | ($ in thousands) | | | |
|  | **Historical cost** | **Replacement cost** | **Asset life** | **Estimated replacement depreciation** |
| Insurance replacement cost estimate[b] | | $488,610 | | |
| Land and improvements | $12,816 | 0 | | |
| Equipment and books | 49,315 | 49,315 | 7 | $7,045 |
| Construction in progress | 18,097 | 18,097 | 35 | 517 |
| Total other than buildings | | 67,412 | | |
| Estimate of buildings replacement cost | 175,985 | 421,198 | 35 | 12,034 |
| Total cost per financial statement footnotes | $256,213 | | | |
| **Estimate of replacement cost depreciation** | | | **C** | $19,596 |

[a] "Payments on long-term debt" from statement of cash flows.

[b] Replacement cost for SanJo University is included in the financial highlights (See Table 8.1.) and in Appendix A, Note 3 (Land, Buildings, and Equipment).

**Ratio 13** Pledges receivable ratio measures the portion of net assets that is made up of the net present value of recorded pledges.

**Pledges receivable ratio =**

| | | 2003 | 2004 | 2005 | 2006 | 2007 |
|---|---|---|---|---|---|---|
| **Pledges receivable** | **A** | 4.81% | 4.49% | 24.98% | 34.43% | 24.46% |
| **Total net assets** | **B** | | | | | |
| | | | | | | |
| Pledges receivable | **A** | $15,285 | $15,333 | $114,800 | $210,875 | $168,214 |
| Total net assets at end of the year | **B** | $317,562 | $341,413 | $459,591 | $612,499 | $687,640 |

because it uses replacement cost depreciation, which is an approximation of the current cost of maintaining and/or replacing an institution's physical plant. While the ratio is very imprecise, over several years it can indicate how well an institution is meeting its capital maintenance needs.

For SanJo, the two ratios give different pictures at the end of 2007. Using historical depreciation, the first ratio equals 192 percent, suggesting the university has $1.92 of operating cash flow for each dollar of capital maintenance. However, using replacement cost depreciation yields a more conservative outcome, with SanJo having 69 cents of operating cash flow for each dollar of capital maintenance. Fortunately, even the more conservative ratio indicates the university has cash flow available for capital maintenance. However, the exact amount needed can only be determined by a more exhaustive study of the university's physical plant.

**Pledges receivable.** This ratio separates pledges from net assets, as pledges do not represent liquid assets at the end of the fiscal year. Pledges should, however, represent future cash flows for the institution. (See Appendix B, Note 2 for a discussion of the calculation of net pledges receivable.) The ratio is

$$\frac{\text{Pledges receivable}}{\text{Total net assets}}$$

The university is well into the collection phase of the major pledges to its capital campaign, and as a result almost 25 percent of its total net assets are pledges that will be collected in the future. This is an unusually high percentage due to the success of the capital campaign.

# Summary

Ratio analysis attempts to capture certain financial constructs related to the college or university. However, it must be remembered that ratios do not provide a complete answer to questions regarding an institution's liquidity, solvency, operating performance, and financial flexibility. Qualitative factors are also important and offer significant information about an institution's financial health. Ratios, however, should serve as "red flags," especially if a ratio is increasing or decreasing significantly or is out of line with the ratios of an institution's peers. Board members who understand the ratios for their institution—and the explanations behind their fluctuations—have a valuable tool at their disposal.

# CHAPTER 8

# Strategic Analysis for Internal Users

In the preceding chapters, we have discussed how to analyze the financial data contained in an institution's annual financial report. In this chapter we focus on how to select and present the appropriate financial and nonfinancial data, so the board can use the resulting report for long-term strategic planning. We tie together financial and nonfinancial indicators, combining ratio analysis from Chapter 7 with the strategic issues raised in Chapter 1. To illustrate the process, we will rely again on our hypothetical institution, SanJo University.

## Selecting Measures

Because college and university financial reports contain so much data, it is important to prioritize the information. The most critical issues are likely to vary from institution to institution. While some institutions may be concerned about their dependence on tuition, others may be more concerned about their level of deferred maintenance and ability to carry additional debt. To complicate matters, the most critical issues for each college or university are likely to change over time. For example, enrollment levels, tuition pricing, and salaries demand attention each year; the progress of a capital campaign is a priority only when the college or university has one.

Together with management, trustees should regularly evaluate which information and measures are most important for their institution. The measures can be financial or nonfinancial; they can come from the financial statements (such as operating ratios) or supplemental information (such as the number of appli-

cations and matriculations in a given year). Finally, they can be quantitative (such as the percentage of applicants admitted) or qualitative (such as demographics of accepted students). Ultimately, these measures should provide valuable information about an institution's financial viability.

By itself, a measure is neither good nor bad. To provide real information, the measures must be compared, either over time or with peer institutions. Consequently, management should track its financial and nonfinancial indicators over several years (which it should already be doing, as financial markets and lenders require longitudinal data, respectively, for certain bond ratings and for meeting established debt covenants). Where possible, management should compare institutional indicators with those of peer colleges or universities, particularly those regarded as the "best in class" for a particular measure or attribute. It is only by comparison that a measure can indicate those areas requiring action.

Once trustees and management determine the priority measures, they must design reports to help monitor them. The reports must:

+ be driven by and relate closely to the institution's mission;

+ use simple graphs and charts that are not overloaded with numbers; and

+ interpret the financial data in each chart and graph clearly and concisely.

The remainder of this chapter looks at key factors that boards of trustees should be familiar with and the types of analyses they can do to better assess the

**Table 8.1** SanJo University statistical abstract featuring financial highlights, 2003 to 2007

|  | **2003** | **2004** | **2005** | **2006** | **2007** |
|---|---|---|---|---|---|
| Total assets | $386,040,000 | $407,935,000 | $542,677,400 | $721,902,910 | $812,532,697 |
| Endowment market value | $215,447,000 | $228,640,000 | $324,116,000 | $443,958,000 | $502,754,000 |
| Plant (land, buildings, and equipment) | $96,211 | $109,626 | $130,240 | $175,000 | $192,999 |
| Total debt outstanding | $49,720 | $48,579 | $62,365 | $85,479 | $97,251 |
|  |  |  |  |  |  |
| Plant replacement value | $222,498,000 | $267,479,803 | $330,066,302 | $421,370,109 | $488,610,020 |
| Gross square feet of buildings | 1,325,500 | 1,497,815 | 1,737,465 | 2,084,958 | 2,272,605 |
| Replacement cost per square foot | $167.86 | $178.58 | $189.97 | $202.10 | $215.00 |
|  |  |  |  |  |  |
| Total private gifts received |  |  |  |  |  |
| Private gifts | $3,147,000 | $3,523,000 | $3,494,000 | $4,029,000 | $4,606,000 |
| Grants | $2,500,000 | $3,200,000 | $3,900,000 | $4,250,000 | $4,502,000 |
| Capital gifts | $12,011,000 | $6,820,000 | $134,098,000 | $159,411,000 | $67,291,000 |
| Total | $17,658,000 | $13,543,000 | $141,492,000 | $167,690,000 | $76,399,000 |
|  |  |  |  |  |  |
| Student aid |  |  |  |  |  |
| University-sponsored financial aid | $6,671,000 | $4,849,000 | $8,484,000 | $9,347,000 | $10,294,000 |
| Donor-sponsored financial aid | $8,892,000 | $9,988,000 | $10,500,000 | $11,000,000 | $11,562,000 |
|  | $15,563,000 | $14,837,000 | $18,984,000 | $20,347,000 | $21,856,000 |
|  |  |  |  |  |  |
| Tuition and fees (including room and board) | $31,700 | $33,400 | $35,200 | $37,000 | $39,000 |
| Average financial aid per student | $9,617 | $9,177 | $11,168 | $11,953 | $12,856 |
| Financial aid as percentage of tuition and fees | 30.3% | 27.5% | 31.7% | 32.3% | 33.0% |
| Percentage of students with university grants | 46.8% | 49.7% | 50.1% | 52.0% | 53.4% |
| Endowment per student | $133,127 | $141,413 | $190,669 | $260,845 | $295,738 |
|  |  |  |  |  |  |
| Student enrollment (FTE) | 1,618 | 1,617 | 1,700 | 1,702 | 1,700 |
| Faculty (FTE) | 114 | 116 | 117 | 119 | 118 |
| Percent tenured | 53.0% | 54.0% | 54.0% | 53.0% | 53.0% |
| Student/faculty ratio | 14.2 | 13.9 | 14.5 | 14.3 | 14.4 |
| Total faculty and staff | 400 | 402 | 401 | 414 | 413 |
|  |  |  |  |  |  |
| Applications for admission | 5,700 | 5,800 | 5,985 | 6,585 | 6,900 |
| Percentage of applicants offered admission | 14.0% | 13.9% | 13.5% | 12.5% | 11.9% |
| Yield on admission offers (% enrolling) | 47.5% | 47.4% | 48.2% | 47.3% | 47.8% |
| Graduation rate | 89.0% | 87.0% | 88.0% | 89.0% | 88.6% |

financial health of the institution. It is an important first step for boards as they plan for the future.

## SanJo University Revisited

Let us turn once again to our hypothetical university, SanJo University. Table 8.1 is a statistical abstract, presenting the institution's financial highlights for the last five years. Like many statistical abstracts, SanJo's contains supplemental data that is often provided in an institution's annual report.

**Applications to SanJo University.** The number of applications that an institution receives is critical in assessing a college's or university's financial health, particularly for those schools that derive a high percentage of their revenues from tuition and fees. Table 8.1 shows that SanJo's FTE student enrollment is 1,700 for the 2006-07 academic year, up from 1,618 FTE students in 2002-03. Its applications for admissions have also grown from 5,700 to 6,900—or 21 percent—over the five-year period. As a result, applicants offered admission has decreased to 11.9 percent, making SanJo a selective institution. Rating agencies look upon increasing applications and decreasing percentages of admission offers as favorable indicators of an institution's long-term financial health. Because applications become enrollments, these admissions ratios are a strong indicator of the institution's ability to continue generating revenue and, more importantly, cash flows in the future.

**Tuition and fees.** SanJo's tuition, fees, room, and board have increased significantly from $31,700 in 2002-03 to $39,000 in 2006-07, making it a relatively expensive independent institution (although not among the most expensive in the United States).[1]

Tuition and fees increased an average of 4 percent annually. In Chapter 7, we calculated SanJo's operating revenue ratio as 73 percent, indicating the university meets 73 percent of its educational and general expenses with its operating revenue. In Chart 8.2, the detailed breakdown of the operating revenue, shows net tuition alone meets 64 percent of the university's educational and general expenses.

**Chart 8.2** Operating revenue ratio: Break down of operating revenue sources

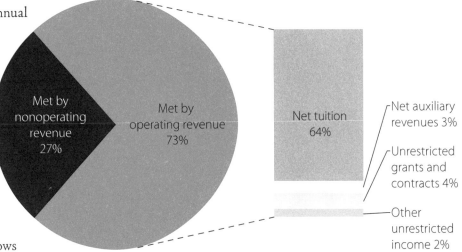

Note: Educational and general expenses total $70 million, as shown in Chapter 7, Ratio 1.

**Tuition dependence.** Clearly, one key issue for SanJo University is its dependence on tuition and, by extension, its ability to attract students. SanJo's trustees may wish to consider the following questions:

- How much has SanJo's tuition increased annually (as a percentage and in dollars)?

- How does the annual tuition increase (percentage) compare with external measures, such as the CPI and the Higher Education Price Index?

- How does the annual tuition increase (percentage) compare with those of SanJo's peers?

- What portion of the increase in tuition revenue is due to enrollment increases versus increases in tuition and fees per student? Can the university continue to increase enrollments to provide more operating revenue?

- How has the university's tuition dependency ratio changed over the last 10 years?

---

[1] Although the statistical abstract for SanJo University does not provide such detail, trustees may want to see tuition and fees and then, separately, the cost of room and board.

- How sensitive is its enrollment to tuition increases?

- What portion of its educational and general expenses does tuition and fees revenue meet?

- How did actual tuition and fees revenue compare with budgeted tuition and fees levels? That is, was the institution able to maintain the enrollment levels it had planned to achieve?

- Could the institution increase the size of its student body beyond its current FTE count? That is, can the university physically accommodate more students in its dormitories? Can it support more students with its current administrative levels? With its current level of faculty?

Few of these questions are easy to answer, and all require substantial analysis. For example, many factors influence the size of the student body, and the price of tuition is only one. The number of applications, the percentage of applications accepted, the enrollment yield, and the retention rate together make up market demand—or the selectivity of the institution—which affects tuition revenue and cash flows. (The bond markets also use SAT and ACT scores, rank in high school class, and other attributes of the student body to measure an institution's selectivity.) The most selective institutions are better able to cope with downturns in the number of applications. In contrast, a highly tuition-dependent institution that must accept a high percentage of applicants is more likely to experience financial difficulty, or at a minimum, a lower degree of financial flexibility.

**Financial aid.** As tuition and fees have escalated and federal grants to students have diminished, financial aid has become an increasingly significant factor in school choice. In fact, many students choose a college or university based on net cost after financial aid. To remain competitive, institutions themselves have had to provide increasing amounts of financial aid. For colleges and universities with sufficient endowment income, this is less of a problem. The greatest difficulty arises when the aid is unfunded.

In Chapter 7, we calculated SanJo's tuition discount ratio at 33 percent, meaning the institution itself supplies one-third of the tuition price to students through financial aid. Close to half of this amount,

15.5 percent, is unfunded aid—in essence, a 15.5 percent tuition discount. Chart 8.3 shows the portion of unfunded aid has increased while the funded portion has decreased over the past five years.

**Chart 8.3** Unfunded versus funded financial aid

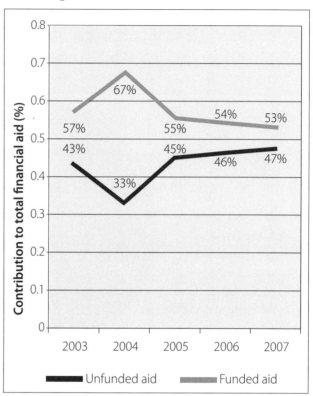

Table 8.1 shows that financial aid increased 40 percent, from $15.6 million in 2002-03 to $21.9 million in 2006-07. Over the same period, tuition, fees, room, and board increased 23 percent. In other words, financial aid grew by a higher percentage than operating revenue. Annually, unfunded aid grew by 9 percent, funded aid by 5.5 percent, and tuition, fees, room, and board by approximately 4 percent.

As a result, the board might want to pursue the following questions with senior management:

- How does the average increase in institutionally funded financial aid compare to the average increase in tuition and fees?

- If the current level of aid continues, what are the university's projected needs for the next five to 10 years? How does this figure compare with projected tuition and fees increases?

* What is SanJo's financial aid packaging strategy?[2]

* Are financial aid applicants "gapped"? That is, is the institution meeting only a portion of each student's full need? What is the trend in the institution's gapping policy?

* How has need-based aid increased compared to merit-based aid? As institutions compete to attract the top students, especially given the importance of various college ratings in school selection, is the institution directing more aid to merit scholarships? How does this shift tie to its overall mission?

* What is the percentage of students on financial aid? What is the size of the average grant? How has the size of the average grant changed over the past 10 years?

* How do the financial aid polices of SanJo University compare to those of its peers?

* Has the increase in its financial aid budget been driven by the nature of SanJo's applicants or by competitive strategies of peer institutions? That is, are more students and parents demanding that SanJo meet the aid awards of other institutions? Are more students and parents expecting merit-based aid as institutions compete for the top students?

**Endowment.** As operating costs have increased faster than inflation, most colleges and universities have increased tuition while also turning to private gifts and endowment income. Gifts, grants, and endowment income increase an institution's operating flexibility, enabling it to leverage other operating revenues, especially tuition. Two key determinants of the flexibility and financial strength of an institution are endowment size and endowment return.[3] An institution can use this income to meet operating expenses, support financial aid, and increase the institution's permanent capital.

For SanJo, the market value of the endowment has increased from $215.4 million in 2002-03 to $502.7 million in 2006-07, an increase of 133 percent. The dramatic improvement is largely the result of SanJo's successful capital campaign. The university's total endowment is over six times the size of its operating expenses ($502.7 million endowment, $82.3 million operating expenses). The higher this ratio, the greater an institution's financial flexibility. While the endowment has grown significantly during the past five years, the investment returns have not been a significant contributor to the overall growth, as we discovered when calculating the total return on the long-term investments ratio in Chapter 7.

The board may want to ask the following questions related to SanJo's endowment:

* What is the institution's endowment-spending policy? That is, how much endowment income and realized gains does the institution allocate to operations?

* Have there been significant differences between the amounts the institution actually spent and the budgeted spending policy amounts?

* What is the total annual return on long-term investments? How does this return compare to the market average? To the return of peer institutions? To its own budget?

* What is the investment strategy of the institution, and what level of risk has it accepted in its portfolio?

* How many of SanJo's alumni donate to the university each year? What is the average size of their gifts?[4]

* How does the institution distinguish between annual giving and incremental giving through capital campaigns?

* Have the university's recent capital campaigns been successful?

* What is the trend in annual giving? What goals has the board established? Has the institution met them?

---

[2] Packaging strategy refers to how a college or university uses institutional and outside resources to meet the financial need of students. Financial need is the cost to attend a particular institution minus the expected family contribution, which is determined by a federal formula.

[3] Many financial strength ratios are based on endowment information, including endowment to operating expenses, quasi endowment to total endowment, endowment per FTE student, and total return on investment. We explained the last two ratios in Chapter 7.

[4] Many rankings of colleges and universities use "percentage of alumni who give" as a surrogate for alumni satisfaction with the institution. Therefore, not only does giving affect operating revenues and endowment, but it also may affect the institution's rankings.

+ What level of financial support have board members made to the institution?

+ What are the institution's efforts toward corporate and foundation gifts?

**Costs.** Over the past decade, expenses for salaries, fringe benefits, and technology have increased much faster than inflation, as institutions have attempted to obtain and retain resources in a competitive marketplace. In the past, colleges and universities passed on these costs to students through double-digit percentage tuition increases. However, in this new era of accountability, cost control is paramount. Many institutions now determine a maximum allowable percentage increase in tuition and fees and then adjust institutional costs to fit.

Consequently, it is important for the board to understand the institution's costs and the key policies affecting them. Remember that the board is responsible for setting and monitoring policies that support the institution's mission. Therefore, they should use financial information to evaluate policies, not to determine them. One way to evaluate costs is to study the statement of activities, because it classifies expenses by functional area, such as institutional and academic support. While this classification provides information about different program costs, it is also beneficial to review expenses according to natural classifications, such as salaries and employee benefits. (See Exhibit D in Chapter 5.) Some institutions use a matrix to compare costs along both functional and natural classifications.

Board members can use the operating ratios we discussed in Chapter 7 to analyze costs and the college or university's ability to cover them. We also recommend the following strategic questions:

+ What are the key expenses driving overall costs (for example, salaries, health care costs, technologies)?

+ How much control does the institution have over these costs, and which ones are driven by external factors? What has been the trend for these expenses over time?

+ How have program costs changed over time? Are more or fewer funds flowing to instructional, research, and support functions?

+ How has the institution fared regarding deferred maintenance? What is the effect of using replacement-cost depreciation when analyzing the amount of cash provided by operations? (See liquidity and cash flow ratios in Chapter 7.)

+ Has the institution drawn on its long-term assets to fund operating expenses?

+ Do auxiliary revenues equal or exceed auxiliary expenses? That is, are housing, food service, and/or bookstore costs fully covered by the revenue they generate?

+ Is the institution adding or deleting programs, and what are the current and future implications of such decisions?

+ How did the university's actual expenses compare with budgeted expenses? What are the causes of any variances?

+ Has the number of university personnel remained constant, or is it increasing or decreasing in different program areas? Has the number of faculty, administrators, and support staff increased over the past five to 10 years? If there is growth, is the university controlling it?[5]

+ How has the student/faculty ratio changed over time? How has this affected costs?

+ What is the average age of the faculty? How many are tenured? What is the impact of retiring faculty on future costs? Is there salary inversion in particular academic disciplines? Will new faculty require salaries significantly higher than those of retiring faculty?

Trustees need comparative, aggregated information to analyze cost issues. However, cost and expense details are not usually available in the financial statements. Therefore, the board may want management to provide supplemental disclosures and reports to the board. Trend information on expenses is central to analyzing the financial health of an institution.

**Use of debt.** When investment returns are a multiple of the institution's incremental borrowing rate, the institution should use such leverage to finance capital

---

5    Because salaries and employee benefits represent the most significant portion of total costs, this information is critical to any cost analysis.

**Table 8.4** Impact of adding debt

| Debt service ratios | 2007 Actual ratio | Pro forma ratio* |
|---|---|---|
| **Debt service to operating expenses ratio** | | |
| $\dfrac{\text{Annual debt service}}{\text{(Operating expenses)} + \text{(Debt principal repayment)}}$ | 7.4% | 8.9% |
| **Debt service coverage ratio** | | |
| $\dfrac{\text{(Operating surplus)} + \text{(Interest expense)}}{\text{Annual debt service}}$ | 87.0% | 70.0% |
| **Total debt to expendable net asset ratios** | | |
| **Expendable unrestricted net assets** | | |
| $\dfrac{\text{Total debt outstanding}}{\text{(Unrestricted net assets)} - \text{(Net investment in plant)}}$ | 94.0% | 113.3% |
| **Expendable net assets** | | |
| $\dfrac{\text{Total debt outstanding}}{\text{(Unrestricted + Temporarily restricted net assets)} - \text{(Net investment in plant)}}$ | 46.9% | 56.5% |

\* This analysis presents a pro forma of what the ratios for SanJo would look like if the university borrowed an additional $20 million and repaid it over 20 years at 4 percent, increasing the annual debt service payments by $1,472,000.

projects. However, most colleges and universities use debt—particularly tax-exempt debt—to finance projects rather than commit other capital resources. This is an especially attractive way to finance self-supporting projects such as dormitories, dining halls, or other revenue-generating facilities. Before deciding to incur any new debt, colleges and universities should assess how they are handling existing debt. Trustees should pay attention to several ratios when considering the effect of new debt on the institution:[6]

+ *Expendable net assets ratios.* What would be the relationship of expendable net assets to operating expenses plus debt service if the institution issued new debt?

+ *Debt service ratios.* What percent of its total operating budget (including required debt principal payments) goes for debt service? What will be the debt coverage ratio with the new debt? Can the

institution still cover all of its debt service requirements with its operating surplus?

+ *Total debt to expendable net assets ratios.* What will be the relationship of the new debt levels to the institution's available expendable unrestricted net assets (unrestricted net assets minus investment in plant)? What will be the relationship of the new debt levels to the institution's expendable net assets (unrestricted net assets plus temporarily restricted net assets minus investment in plant)?

Turning again to SanJo University, let us look at the effect of issuing $20 million of debt over 20 years, assuming a borrowing cost of 4 percent. The annual debt service would be $1.47 million, which would affect each of SanJo's key ratios.

The new debt service—at almost 9 percent of operating costs—would have a significant impact on the budget. Both the actual and pro forma debt service coverage ratios would be below 100 percent, which

---

[6] Using quasi endowment instead of financing a project also affects several ratios.

indicates the institution is unable to meet its debt obligations from current operating resources. Outstanding debt would increase dramatically in relation to expendable net assets. This analysis does not necessarily mean the university should not borrow more. Rather, it should help trustees frame their decisions in the context of the university's other long-term needs while they carefully evaluate how to repay this debt.

## Summary

Identifying the key issues and related financial indicators for your institution is the first important step in measuring progress. Trustees and administrators must agree on the issues and measures they will routinely review at meetings of the board or its finance committee. The information should include trends for several accounting periods, and it periodically should be compared with data from peer institutions, with regional and national averages, and with institutions considered "best in class."

Asking the right questions and understanding the answers is essential. The questions presented throughout this chapter provide a starting point for trustees, while ratio analysis provides a useful tool for capturing and interpreting financial data. Ultimately, the goal of this book is to help boards and managers make the strategic decisions necessary for the survival and growth of their colleges and universities.

# CHAPTER 9

# Audit Committee Responsibility for Financial Reporting

We began this book with a discussion of the Sarbanes-Oxley Act of 2002, which transformed the external reporting process. In particular, audit committees must now have at least one financial expert to ensure the committee is capable of exercising appropriate oversight. However, for colleges and universities, finding financial experts can be difficult, as few specialize in reporting for not-for-profit organizations. Even when an audit committee does have a financial expert, it is in the institution's best interest to ensure the entire committee has an understanding of college and university financial statements and specific knowledge about the institution's reporting practices and financial issues. The goal of this chapter, then, is to address audit committees and their responsibility to ensure that the institution issues informative, meaningful financial reports.

The audit committee's responsibilities fall into six major areas:

**Table 9.1** Audit committee responsibilities

(1) Managing the relationship with the external auditors
- Appoint, compensate, and evaluate the independent external auditor
- Review auditor independence
- Act on audit findings

(2) Ensuring the quality of financial reporting
- Evaluate the quality of reporting
- Inquire about disclosures, including management discussion and analysis

(3) Overseeing regulatory compliance
- Ensure compliance with laws and GAAP

(4) Working with the internal auditors
- Oversee charter, authority, and resources
- Review audit scope
- Ensure effectiveness
- Evaluate performance

(5) Assessing management's performance with internal controls and risk management
- Understand risk areas
- Oversee effectiveness of controls

(6) Monitoring ethics program
- Administer codes of conduct and conflicts of interest
- Oversee system for addressing complaints (for example, whistleblowers)

*Source:* John A. Mattie and John H. McCarthy, "The Changing Role of the Audit Committee: Leading Practices for Colleges, Universities, and Other Not-for-Profit Education Institutions," white paper (PricewaterhouseCoopers, 2004),

The following discussion focuses on the second point, "Ensuring the quality of financial reporting." We pose 30 questions that board or audit committee members should be able to answer after reading the institution's financial statements. These questions assume the financial statements do indeed provide a full and transparent accounting for the institution and that board members have a basic understanding of college and university financial statements. The answers will come from information on the statements themselves, management discussion and analysis (MD&A), or discussions with management and/or the external auditors.[1]

---

[1] MD&A is a formal discussion of the institution's financial performance over the reporting period. While there are no requirements for independent colleges and universities to include MD&A, many add it voluntarily to enhance reporting transparency.

# General Questions about the Financial Report

(1) Does the annual financial report include an MD&A on the results of operations and other major changes for the year?

(2) Does the MD&A provide a clear and concise explanation of the institution's financial condition at its year-end?

(3) Does the MD&A include forward-looking information about upcoming significant events that will affect the institution?

(4) Is the auditors' report on the financial statements free of any qualifications or other unusual language? If not, why not?

(5) What areas in the financial statements involve significant management estimates? (These areas usually include reserves for potentially uncollectible accounts, notes or pledges receivable, valuation of certain nonmarketable investments, and reserves for various contingencies such as unresolved regulatory reviews or outstanding litigation.) Is this made clear in the footnotes?

# Questions about the Statement of Financial Position and Related Footnotes

(1) What are the most significant assets? (Usually, they include land, buildings, equipment, and long-term investments.)

(2) What are the most significant liabilities? (These usually are long-term debt, pension, and other post-retirement benefit accruals.)

(3) Does the college or university have any unusual categories of assets or liabilities? What are they and how did they arise?

(4) Do the footnotes sufficiently explain which assets the institution actually held and how well the long-term investments performed?

(5) Are the amounts of significant reserves for uncollectible accounts, notes or pledges, liabilities, and contingencies readily apparent?

# Questions about the Statement of Activities and Related Footnotes

Recall that changes in net assets for the year result from three major activities:

+ *Operations*, which for most colleges and universities produce small surpluses or losses;

+ *Investments*, which involves the whole investment management process; and

+ *Fundraising*, which includes nonoperating fundraising, usually for new facilities, endowment, or some other donor-restricted purpose (such as future student financial aid or program support).

With this in mind, the key questions about the statement of activities include:

(1) How much of tuition and fee revenue was available for operations? How much was, in effect, abated in the form of financial aid? How much of the financial aid was funded (that is, donor-sponsored) versus pure discount?

(2) Do auxiliary enterprises break even or show a small profit?

(3) Are there significant year-to-year fluctuations in the other major revenue sources? If so, are the reasons apparent from the statement or footnotes?

(4) Was there a surplus from operating activities?

(5) Can you easily tell what the total return on investments was? How much was used for operating activities (that is, the spending rate)? How much was reinvested?

(6) Can you easily tell how much donor support the college or university received during the period? How much was used for operations? How much was reinvested?

(7) Were the changes in unrestricted, temporarily restricted, and permanently restricted net assets positive?

(8) Did total net assets increase by more than the rate of inflation during the period? In other words, was there real growth in the total net assets?

## Questions about the Statement of Cash Flows and Related Footnotes

(1) Do the operating activities provide or consume cash?

(2) If operations consumed cash, does it appear to be a temporary situation or a structural problem?

(3) Are the cash flows from, or for, investing activities consistent with your understanding of how the institution is investing in its future?

(4) Are the financing cash flows consistent with your understanding of how the institution is using debt and/or fundraising to finance its investing activities?

(5) Is the overall cash flow positive? If not, why not?

(6) Are the amounts held in cash and cash equivalents reasonable in relation to prior year end balances?

## Questions for the Auditors

Under generally accepted auditing standards, external auditors must make certain required communications with the board or its audit committee in writing. Several of these required communications address matters that could affect the quality of the financial reporting process. Briefly, the required communications include:

- Any change in a client's *accounting policies or methods* used to account for significant or unusual transactions. The goal is to assure the board that consistent and appropriate accounting practices were used.

- The nature of *significant management estimates* used to prepare the financial statements and the auditors' conclusion about how reasonable the estimates are. The goal is to assure the board that such estimates are justifiable and appropriately documented.

- Any *significant accounting adjustments* made—or proposed adjustments that were not made—to the financial statements as a result of the audit process. The goal is to inform the board about the quality of management's accounting process and assure that all appropriate adjustments have been made in the financial statements.

- Other issues, such as the auditors' responsibility in the performance of an audit, any disagreements the auditors had with management, attempts by management to seek advice from other auditors (known as "opinion shopping"), or any difficulties with management that might affect the audit.

It also would be prudent for the audit committee to question the auditor about any error corrections or restatements.

In addition to carefully reviewing all the formal reports provided by the independent auditors, the board or audit committee should always request a meeting with the auditors without members of management present (that is, in executive session). In an executive session board members would be wise to ask the following questions:

(1) What is your assessment of the financial management team and their ability to produce reliable and timely financial reports? This is also an opportunity for board members to ask about specific team members about whom they have concerns.

(2) How aggressive are the institution's revenue recognition practices?

(3) How conservative are the institution's practices for establishing reserves for liabilities and contingencies?

(4) If the audited financial statements were not available within 90 days of the institution's fiscal year-end, why did they take longer to prepare?

(5) How adequate are the systems that support the financial reporting process?

(6) What questions should we have asked that might shed further light on the quality of the institution's financial reporting process? How would you answer those questions?

The foregoing list of questions is by no means exhaustive. There are many other questions that board members could—and depending on the situation, should—ask when assessing the quality of the reporting process. The answers to these questions should serve as a solid basic assessment of the college or university's quality of external financial reporting.

## Summary

The goal of this text has been to explain how to read basic financial statements of independent colleges and universities and how to use financial ratios to evaluate the information contained in them. We have suggested strategic questions that can help independent college and university boards and management assess the effectiveness of the institution's financial operations and the quality of its financial reporting process. Ultimately, the financial reporting process should help explain and support the mission of the institution and allow the board and external users to make informed decisions about the institution. We hope this book proves to be a useful tool in this process.

# SanJo University Financial Highlights and Financial Statements

*For the year ended June 30, 2007 (with summarized financial information for 2006)[1]*

## Financial Highlights

The university continues to reap the benefits from its $380 million "Campaign for Tomorrow," having already received $354 million in gifts and pledges with a year still remaining in the campaign. These new resources have affected every aspect of the university's operations and dramatically improved its financial position. In 2007, net assets increased 12 percent to $688 million, and over the past five years net assets have grown by $370 million, an increase of 117 percent.

## Operating Activities

The primary source of the university's operating revenues continues to be net tuition and fees, which fund 64 percent of its educational and general expenses (excluding auxiliary enterprises). After adjusting for student financial aid granted, tuition and fees have increased an average of 5.6 percent annually over the past five years. In 2007, private gifts and grants grew

over 10 percent to $9.1 million, and investment income used for operations under the university's spending formula grew 8 percent to $13.6 million.

The university is committed to providing an outstanding education at an affordable price. As a result student financial aid continues to increase. In 2007, over half of our students received direct financial aid from the university amounting to 33 percent of gross tuition and fees. While total tuition and fees to attend SanJo University grew to $39,000, on average students and their families actually paid $26,100.

Operating expenses grew another 6.1 percent in 2007. The university has successfully attracted and retained faculty who are leaders in their respective academic fields, but the ongoing competition for top faculty has contributed significantly to our operating costs. Skyrocketing technology costs have also affected the operating budget. Despite these cost pressures, the operating margin was $4.1 million or 4.8 percent of operating revenues in 2007 and has averaged 6 percent over the past five years.

## Endowment and Investments

The university's long-term investments grew 38 percent to $416.5 million as the result of capital contributions and a modest investment return of 4.2 percent. Investment returns were influenced by the timing of certain private equity investments. The invested endowment grew 43 percent to $342.5 million in 2007. Total endowment and similar funds reached an all-

---

[1] The purpose of the financial statements and related notes is to provide a basic understanding of financial reporting for determining financial ratios. The financial statements and notes are not meant to be a complete presentation in accordance with generally accepted accounting principles, or contain disclosures related to financial accounting standards and interpretations issued subsequent to the date of these example financial statements.

time high of $502.7 million (including $168.2 million in pledges) or $295,738 per student. The endowment payout provided $13.6 million or 16 percent of the university's total operating revenues.

## Facilities

In the past five years the university has expended $147.5 million on new facilities, funded by the proceeds of "Campaign for Tomorrow" and also new debt. This investment has changed the face of SanJo University. The new Martell Science Center has added laboratory space to expand the biology and chemistry programs. The Wentzel Athletic Forum provides improved facilities for intercollegiate and intramural athletics as well as a new fitness center for the entire campus community. The addition of the DeAcetis, Gaudrault, and Pike dormitories now enables us to offer on-campus housing to all students.

## Debt

The university continues to avail itself of tax-exempt debt issued through the State Education Finance Authority, significantly reducing the cost of borrowing. Our new facilities were financed in part with $47.5 million of net new debt, yet the average interest paid was just 3.37 percent in 2007. The debt service coverage ratio was 108 percent in 2006 but fell to 87 percent in 2007.

## Overall Financial Position

The university remains in a strong financial position. The total endowment and similar funds—excluding unpaid pledges—is over 400 percent of total operating costs. With current assets at more than 200 percent of current liabilities, the university has a solid working capital position. With the expected collection of $168.2 million in additional pledges over the next seven years, the university financial position should only get stronger.

**Exhibit A** SanJo University statement of financial position, FY 2007 and FY 2006

**SanJo University
Statement of Financial Position**

For the two years ended June 30, 2007 and 2006 (in thousands)

| | 2007 | 2006 |
|---|---|---|
| **Assets** | | |
| Cash and cash equivalents | $14,200 | $14,225 |
| Accounts receivable, net | 1,700 | 1,650 |
| Short-term investments | 10,925 | 10,850 |
| Inventories | 1,380 | 1,325 |
| Prepaid expenses and other assets | 2,518 | 2,425 |
| Pledges receivable, net | 168,214 | 210,875 |
| Student loans receivable, net | 4,131 | 3,592 |
| Long-term investments, at market | 416,466 | 301,961 |
| Land, buildings, and equipment, net | 192,999 | 175,000 |
| Total assets | $812,533 | $721,903 |
| | | |
| **Liabilities** | | |
| Accounts payable and accrued expenses | $8,977 | $7,800 |
| Deposits and deferred revenues | 4,760 | 4,033 |
| Postretirement benefits | 9,799 | 8,548 |
| Federal student loan funds | 4,106 | 3,544 |
| Long-term debt | 97,251 | 85,479 |
| Total liabilities | $124,893 | $109,404 |
| | | |
| **Net assets** | | |
| Unrestricted | | |
| Funds functioning as endowment | $79,079 | $77,874 |
| Investment in plant, net of long-term debt | 95,748 | 89,521 |
| Undesignated | 24,373 | 16,019 |
| Unrestricted total | 199,200 | 183,414 |
| Temporarily restricted | 103,976 | 99,912 |
| Permanently restricted | 384,464 | 329,173 |
| Total net assets | $687,640 | $612,499 |
| | | |
| Total liabilities and net assets | $812,533 | $721,903 |

**Exhibit B** SanJo University statement of activities, FY 2007 and FY 2006

**SanJo University**
**Statement of Activities**

For the two years ended June 30, 2007 and 2006 (in thousands)

| | Unrestricted | Temporarily restricted | Permanently restricted | Totals 2007 | 2006 |
|---|---|---|---|---|---|
| **Operating revenues** | | | | | |
| Tuition and fees | $66,300 | | | $66,300 | $62,985 |
| University-sponsored financial aid | (10,294) | | | (10,294) | (9,347) |
| Donor-sponsored financial aid | (11,562) | | | (11,562) | (11,000) |
| Net tuition and fees | 44,444 | | | 44,444 | 42,638 |
| Sales and services of auxiliaries | 14,807 | | | 14,807 | 14,101 |
| Government grants and contracts | 2,750 | | | 2,750 | 2,633 |
| Private gifts and grants | 5,436 | 3,672 | | 9,108 | 8,279 |
| Investment income used for operations | 13,594 | | | 13,594 | 12,569 |
| Other income | 1,750 | | | 1,750 | 1,590 |
| Net assets released from restrictions | 1,908 | (1,908) | | | |
| Total operating revenues | $84,689 | $1,764 | | $86,453 | $81,810 |
| **Operating expenses** | | | | | |
| Instruction and research | 37,062 | | | 37,062 | 35,090 |
| Libraries | 4,401 | | | 4,401 | 3,972 |
| Academic support | 7,852 | | | 7,852 | 7,398 |
| Student services | 7,504 | | | 7,504 | 7,070 |
| General administration | 13,132 | | | 13,132 | 12,372 |
| Auxiliaries enterprises | 12,357 | | | 12,357 | 11,642 |
| Total operating expenses | $82,308 | | | $82,308 | $77,544 |
| Increase in net assets from operating activities | $2,381 | $1,764 | | $4,145 | $4,266 |
| **Nonoperating activities** | | | | | |
| Total investment income | 8,207 | 6,892 | | 15,099 | 7,684 |
| Less investment income used for operations | (9,002) | (4,592) | | (13,594) | (12,569) |
| Capital gifts | 2,000 | 10,000 | 55,291 | 67,291 | 159,411 |
| Other | 2,200 | | | 2,200 | (5,884) |
| Net assets released from restrictions | 10,000 | (10,000) | | | |
| Increase in net assets from nonoperating activities | $13,405 | $2,300 | $55,291 | $70,996 | $148,642 |
| Net increase in net assets | 15,786 | 4,064 | 55,291 | 75,141 | 152,908 |
| Net assets at beginning of year | 183,414 | 99,912 | 329,173 | 612,499 | 459,591 |
| Net assets at end of year | $199,200 | $103,976 | $384,464 | $687,640 | $612,499 |

**Exhibit C** SanJo University statement of cash flows, FY 2007 and FY 2006

**SanJo University**
**Statement of Cash Flows**

For the two years ended June 30, 2007 and 2006 (in thousands)

| | 2007 | 2006 |
|---|---:|---:|
| **Cash flows from operating activities** | | |
| Change in net assets | $75,141 | $152,908 |
| Adjustments to reconcile change in net assets | | |
| to net cash provided by operating activities: | | |
| Depreciation | 7,001 | 5,240 |
| (Gains) losses on investments | (6,040) | 252 |
| Capital gifts | (105,000) | (65,000) |
| Changes in assets and liabilities that provide (use) cash: | | |
| Accounts receivable | (50) | (130) |
| Short-term investments | (75) | (330) |
| Inventories | (55) | (68) |
| Prepaid expenses and other assets | (93) | (238) |
| Pledges receivable | 42,661 | (96,075) |
| Student loans receivable | (539) | (469) |
| Accounts payable and accrued expenses | 1,177 | 1,012 |
| Deposits and deferred revenues | 727 | 614 |
| Postretirement benefits | 1,251 | 1,089 |
| Other changes | 562 | 489 |
| Net cash provided by (used for) operating activities | $16,668 | ($706) |
| **Cash flows from investing activities** | | |
| Purchases of plant and equipment, net | (25,000) | (50,000) |
| Purchases of investments | (321,624) | (265,814) |
| Proceeds from sales and maturities of investments | 213,159 | 228,131 |
| Net cash used in investing activities | ($133,465) | ($87,683) |
| **Cash flows from financing activities** | | |
| Proceeds from contributions for: | | |
| Investment in endowment | 95,000 | 40,000 |
| Investment in long-lived assets | 10,000 | 25,000 |
| Proceeds from issuance of long-term debt | 15,000 | 25,000 |
| Payments on long-term debt | (3,228) | (1,886) |
| Net cash provided by financing activities | $116,772 | $88,114 |
| Net decrease in cash and cash equivalents | (25) | (275) |
| Cash and cash equivalents, beginning of year | 14,225 | 14,500 |
| Cash and cash equivalents, end of year | $14,200 | $14,225 |
| **Supplemental data** | | |
| Interest paid | $3,078 | $2,749 |

**Exhibit D** SanJo University statement of functional expenses, FY 2007 and FY 2006

**SanJo University**
**Statement of Functional Expenses**

For the years ended June 30, 2007 and 2006 (in thousands)

| | Instruction and research | Libraries | Academic support | Student services | General admin | Auxiliary enterprises | Total expenses |
|---|---|---|---|---|---|---|---|
| **2007** | | | | | | | |
| Salaries and benefits | $25,202 | $2,993 | $5,339 | $5,103 | $8,930 | $8,403 | $55,969 |
| Purchased services | 3,150 | 374 | 667 | 638 | 1,116 | 1,050 | 6,996 |
| Supplies and general | 1,112 | 132 | 236 | 225 | 394 | 371 | 2,469 |
| Utilities | 1,853 | 220 | 393 | 375 | 657 | 618 | 4,115 |
| Travel | 741 | 88 | 157 | 150 | 263 | 247 | 1,646 |
| Other expenses | 465 | 55 | 99 | 94 | 165 | 155 | 1,033 |
| Depreciation | 3,152 | 374 | 668 | 638 | 1,117 | 1,051 | 7,001 |
| Interest | 1,386 | 165 | 294 | 281 | 491 | 462 | 3,078 |
| | $37,062 | $4,401 | $7,852 | $7,504 | $13,132 | $12,357 | $82,308 |
| **2006** | | | | | | | |
| Salaries and benefits | $24,367 | $2,700 | $5,126 | $4,899 | $8,572 | $8,067 | $53,730 |
| Purchased services | 3,196 | 379 | 677 | 647 | 1,132 | 1,065 | 7,097 |
| Supplies and general | 1,048 | 124 | 222 | 212 | 371 | 349 | 2,326 |
| Utilities | 1,746 | 207 | 370 | 353 | 619 | 582 | 3,877 |
| Travel | 698 | 83 | 148 | 141 | 247 | 233 | 1,551 |
| Other expenses | 438 | 52 | 93 | 89 | 155 | 146 | 973 |
| Depreciation | 2,359 | 280 | 500 | 478 | 836 | 787 | 5,240 |
| Interest | 1,238 | 147 | 263 | 251 | 439 | 413 | 2,749 |
| | $35,090 | $3,972 | $7,398 | $7,070 | $12,372 | $11,642 | $77,544 |

*Because of rounding, totals are not exact.

# Notes to Financial Statements

## 1. *Summary of Significant Accounting Policies*

### (a) Basis of Presentation

The financial statements of SanJo University use the accrual basis of accounting in accordance with generally accepted accounting principles for not-for-profit organizations. The amounts presented in the footnotes are in thousands of dollars unless otherwise noted.

For accounting purposes, resources are reported in separate classes of net assets based on the existence or absence of donor-imposed restrictions. In the accompanying financial statements, net assets with similar characteristics have been combined into categories as follows:

> *Permanently restricted net assets* have donor-imposed stipulations that they be maintained permanently by the university, and primarily include the university's permanent endowment fund. Generally, donors permit the university to use all or part of the investment return on these assets.

> *Temporarily restricted net assets* have donor-imposed stipulations that can be fulfilled by actions of the university pursuant to those stipulations or that expire with the passage of time.

> *Unrestricted net assets* are not subject to donor-imposed stipulations. Unrestricted net assets, however, may be designated for specific purposes by the Board of Trustees or may otherwise be limited by contractual agreements with outside parties.

Revenues are reported as increases in unrestricted net assets unless their use is limited by donor-imposed restrictions. Revenues associated with research and grants are recognized when the related costs are incurred.

Expenses are generally reported as decreases in unrestricted net assets. Realized and unrealized gains and losses on investments and other assets (or liabilities) are reported as increases (or decreases) in unrestricted net assets unless their use is restricted by explicit donor stipulation or by law. Expirations of donor-imposed stipulations that simultaneously increase one class of net assets and decrease another are identified as "Net assets released from restrictions" and reported as reclassifications between the applicable classes of net assets.

The cost of providing various programs and activities has been summarized on a functional basis in the Statement of Activities and the Statement of Functional Expenses. Accordingly, certain costs have been allocated among the programs and supporting services benefited, based on direct costs, usage, and other factors.

Contributions, including unconditional pledges, are recognized as revenues in the period received. Conditional pledges are not recognized until the university substantially meets the conditions on which they depend. Gifts of securities are recorded at their fair market value when received. Pledges are recorded net of an allowance for amounts estimated to be uncollectible and a discount to reflect the present value of the expected future cash amounts to be received.

Contributions and investment returns with donor-imposed restrictions are reported as temporarily restricted revenues and are released to unrestricted net assets when the restriction is satisfied. Contributions restricted for the acquisition of land, buildings, and equipment are reported as temporarily restricted revenues. These contributions are released to unrestricted net assets when the assets are placed in service.

Nonoperating activities include investing activity except when the investment income and gains are used to support operations. Nonoperating activities also include transactions of a capital nature (for example, contributions designated for facilities and equipment or invested to generate a return to support future operations) and other nonrecurring transactions.

### (b) Investments

The university accounts for its investments at fair value, and accordingly, the carrying amount approximates fair value. Earnings on investments as well as the net appreciation (or depreciation) in the fair value of investments, which consists of the realized gains or losses and the unrealized appreciation (or depreciation) on those investments, is shown in the Statement of Activities as total return on investment income. (See also Note 4.) The average cost of investment securities sold is used to determine the basis for computing realized gains and losses.

The value of publicly traded fixed income and equity securities is based on quoted market prices and exchange rates, if applicable. The fair value of significant real estate investments is determined from valuations prepared by independent appraisers. Limited partnership interests, private equities, and certain other nonmarketable securities are valued using the most current information available, generally obtained from the general partner or investment manager for the respective investments.

### (c) Endowment Investment Return Spending Policy

The university has an endowment and similar funds investment return spending policy, which permits spending at 5 percent of the trailing average fair value of the endowment for the preceding 12 quarters. Any income earned in excess of the spending limit is reinvested, while funds may be withdrawn from investment return earned in prior years if its income is less than the board-approved spending limit.

### (d) Inventories

Inventories are stated at the lower of cost (first-in, first-out method) or fair value.

### (e) Student Loan Receivable

Student loan receivable at June 30, 2007 and 2006 are reported net of provisions for doubtful loans of $485,000 and $395,000, respectively. The provision covers loans, both in repayment status and not yet in repayment status (borrowers still in school or in the grace period following graduation), that may not be collected. Notes receivable are mostly amounts due from students under federally sponsored loan programs, which are subject to significant restrictions. Accordingly, it is not practicable to determine the fair value of such amounts.

### (f) Land, Buildings, and Equipment

Land, buildings, and equipment are recorded at cost, or if donated, at fair value on the date of donation. Interest incurred on funds borrowed for facilities construction is capitalized until the assets are placed in service. Depreciation is computed on a straight-line basis over the estimated useful lives of the related assets as follows:

|  | **Years** |
| --- | --- |
| Land improvements | 7–10 |
| Buildings and improvements | 20–50 |
| Equipment and library books | 3–10 |

## (g) Cash Equivalents

Cash equivalents include short-term, highly liquid investments with a maturity of three months or less when purchased. Temporary cash and cash equivalents invested as part of the university's endowment and similar funds, and annuity and life income funds are included in long-term investments. Cash and cash equivalents are reported at cost, which approximates fair value.

## (h) Internal Revenue Code Status

The university has been granted tax-exempt status as a non-profit organization under Section 501(c)(3) of the Internal Revenue Code.

## (i) Use of Estimates

The preparation of financial statements in accordance with generally accepted accounting principles requires management to make estimates and assumptions that affect the reported amounts of assets and liabilities at the date of the financial statements and the reported amounts of revenues and expenses during the period. Actual results could differ from those estimates.

## 2. *Pledges Receivable*

The university has raised $354 million toward its 2008 capital campaign goal of $380 million. Pledges outstanding at June 30, 2007 and 2006 are summarized as follows:

|  | 2007 | 2006 |
|---|---|---|
| Pledges expected to be collected: |  |  |
| Less than one year | $103,476 | $116,725 |
| One year to five years | 75,297 | 104,498 |
| More than five years | 7,198 | 14,974 |
| Total gross pledges | 185,971 | 236,197 |
| Less:    Allowance for uncollectible amounts | (5,579) | (7,086) |
|          Discount to present value | (12,178) | (18,236) |
| Total pledges, net | $168,214 | $210,875 |
|  |  |  |
| Total cash contributions received | $71,615 | $119,060 |
| Regular fundraising costs | $1,363 | $1,333 |
| Capital campaign costs | $6,256 | $2,612 |

The discount to present value was calculated using a discount factor based on U.S. Treasury note rates for the respective pledges. Regular fundraising costs are included with general administration costs, while costs associated directly with the capital campaign are netted against capital gifts as the costs are incurred.

## 3. Land, Buildings, and Equipment

Investment in land, buildings, and equipment consists of the following at June 30:

|  | 2007 | 2006 |
|---|---|---|
| Land and improvements | $12,816 | $10,816 |
| Buildings | 175,985 | 168,891 |
| Equipment and books | 49,315 | 45,264 |
| Construction in progress | 18,097 | 6,242 |
|  | 256,213 | 231,213 |
| Less: Accumulated depreciation | (63,214) | (56,213) |
|  | $192,999 | $175,000 |
|  |  |  |
| Depreciation expense | $7,001 | $5,240 |

## 4. Investments

Investments are stated at fair value. Long-term investments consist of the following as of June 30:

|  | 2007 | | 2006 | |
|---|---|---|---|---|
|  | Cost | Fair Value | Cost | Fair Value |
| Cash equivalents | $19,486 | $19,486 | $36,892 | $36,892 |
| Fixed income | 150,215 | 150,384 | 87,954 | 88,521 |
| Common stock | 111,209 | 103,574 | 108,083 | 102,317 |
| Limited partnerships and other | 71,453 | 97,205 | 31,897 | 45,615 |
| Real estate | 31,116 | 45,817 | 22,495 | 28,616 |
|  | $383,479 | $416,466 | $287,321 | $301,961 |

Short-term investments include mostly securities with maturities of up to three years at the time of purchase.

The components of total investment income from all sources for 2007 and 2006, net of related management and custodial expenses of $4.847 and $3.947 million, respectively, were:

|  | 2007 | 2006 |
|---|---|---|
| Investment income: |  |  |
| Dividends and interest income | $9,059 | $7,936 |
| Realized gains (losses) on investments | (12,307) | 2,224 |
| Unrealized gains (losses) on investments | 18,347 | (2,476) |
| Total return | $15,099 | $7,684 |
|  |  |  |
| Investment income used for operations: |  |  |
| Dividends and interest income | $9,059 | $7,936 |
| Accumulated gains used | 4,535 | 4,633 |
| Total spending formula amount used | $13,594 | $12,569 |

Investment income used for operations in 2006 required the use of accumulated gains earned in previous years, because total investment income for 2006 was less than the board-approved spending formula amount for the year.

**Pooled Funds.** Endowment and similar funds assets are pooled on a unit fair value basis whenever possible. Funds are added to or withdrawn from the pool at the unit fair value at the beginning of the fiscal quarter in which the transaction takes place. The following is a summary, in actual dollar amounts, of the pooled endowment funds for the years ended June 30:

|  | 2007 | 2006 |
|---|---|---|
| Pooled endowment and similar funds at fair value | $342,513,000 | $238,958,000 |
| Endowment shares outstanding | 2,060,686 | 1,503,912 |
| Fair value per share | $166.21 | $158.89 |
| Total investment income per share | $7.33 | $5.11 |

## 5. Long-Term Obligations

Long-term obligations of plant funds at June 30 are summarized as follows:

|  | 2007 | 2006 |
|---|---|---|
| State Education Finance Authority Debt |  |  |
| Series A, 5.0% due 2009 | $13,000 | $14,000 |
| Series B, 4.5% due 2020 | 5,000 | 5,000 |
| Series C, 2.5% due 2025 | 40,000 | 40,000 |
| Series D, 3.0% due 2026 | 25,000 | 25,000 |
| Series E, 3.0% due 2027 | 13,000 |  |
| Equipment Notes, various terms (average 5%) | 1,251 | 1,479 |
|  | $97,251 | $85,479 |

Based on current rates of debts with terms and remaining maturities similar to the university's, the estimated fair value of the university's total existing debt approximates its carrying amount.

The various notes and bonds are collateralized by the related property and equipment as well as certain pledges of tuition and fees. Most of the agreements require the university to maintain certain debt coverage ratios. The university is in compliance with all debt covenant requirements. Principal maturities of the long-term obligations are due as follows:

| 2008 | $1,500 |
|---|---|
| 2009 | 12,751 |
| After 2012 | 83,000 |
| Total debt outstanding | $97,251 |

## 6. Benefits Plans

The university has a defined contribution retirement plan, administered by an independent trustee, for all employees who have completed one year of service. All retirement benefits are funded and vested under a defined contribution program. The university's contributions to the plan totaled approximately $2.549 and $2.462 million in 2007 and 2006, respectively.

The university provides certain health care benefits for retired employees who meet age and service requirements. Employees will become eligible for those benefits if they reach retirement age while employed by the university. The plan is funded as claims are paid. The university accounts for these benefits under SFAS No. 106, "Employers' Accounting for Post-retirement Benefits Other Than Pensions." The estimated future cost of providing post-retirement health care benefits is recognized on an accrual basis over the period of service during which benefits are earned.

The net post-retirement health care benefits cost was determined as follows:

|  | 2007 | 2006 |
|---|---|---|
| Service cost | $600 | $666 |
| Interest cost | 605 | 640 |
| Amortization of prior service cost | 125 | 0 |
| Amortization of loss | 226 | 73 |
| Net periodic post-retirement benefit cost | $1,556 | $1,379 |

The components of the university's accumulated post-retirement benefits obligation, which was unfunded at year end, are as follows:

|  | 2007 | 2006 |
|---|---|---|
| Accumulated post-retirement benefit obligation | $11,139 | $11,723 |
| Unrecognized net loss from past experience difference from that assumed and from changes in assumptions | (2,180) | (4,140) |
| Unrecognized net prior service cost | 840 | 965 |
| Accrued post-retirement benefit cost | $9,799 | $8,548 |

For measurement purposes, a 9 percent annual increase in the per capita cost of covered health care benefits for post-65 benefits was assumed for FY 2008. The rate was assumed to decrease gradually to 5 percent for FY 2014 and remain at that level thereafter. An 8.5 percent annual increase in the per capita cost of covered health care benefits for the pre-65 benefits was assumed for FY 2008. The rate was assumed to decrease gradually to 5 percent for FY 2014 and remain at that level thereafter. A 9.5 percent annual increase in the Medicare Part D subsidy integration threshold was assumed for FY 2008. The rate was assumed to decrease gradually to 5 percent for FY 2014 and remain at that level thereafter.

A 1 percent increase in the assumed health care cost trend rate would have increased the accumulated benefits obligation by $1.504 million at June 30, 2007 and the service and interest costs of the net periodic post-retirement benefits for the year then ended by $0.227 million. Likewise, a 1 percent decrease in the assumed health care cost trend rate would have decreased the accumulated post-retirement benefits obligation by $1.255 million at June 30, 2007 and the service and interest costs of the net periodic post-retirement benefits for the year then ended by $0.183 million. The discount rate used to determine the accumulated benefits obligations was 6.25 percent and 5.5 percent at June 30, 2007 and 2006, respectively.

A reconciliation of the accumulated post-retirement benefits obligation and plan assets are as follows at June 30:

|  | 2007 | 2006 |
|---|---|---|
| Reconciliation of benefits obligation: | | |
| Benefit obligations, beginning of year | $8,548 | $7,259 |
| Service cost | 600 | 666 |
| Interest cost | 605 | 640 |
| Plan benefit contributions | 33 | 27 |
| Actuarial (gain) loss | 400 | 1,618 |
| Plan amendments | 0 | (1,256) |
| Benefits paid | (387) | (406) |
| Benefit obligations, end of year | $9,799 | $8,548 |
| | | |
| Reconciliation of plan assets: | | |
| Fair value of plan assets, beginning of year | $0 | $0 |
| Actual return on plan assets | 0 | 0 |
| Employer contributions (net of expected Medicare Plan D subsidy) | 354 | 378 |
| Plan participant contributions | 33 | 27 |
| Benefits paid | (387) | (405) |
| Fair value of plan assets, end of year | $0 | $0 |

On December 8, 2003, Congress enacted the Medicare Prescription Drug, Improvement and Moderniza-tion Act of 2003 (Public Law 108-173). The university's Post-Retirement Medical Benefits Program is actuari-ally equivalent to Medicare Part D. As such, the calculation of the annual net periodic post-retirement benefit cost and the accumulated post-retirement benefit obligation reflect the expected subsidy from Medicare Part D. Expected Medicare Part D subsidies are as follows (in actual dollars):

| | | | |
|---|---|---|---|
| **2008** | $58,250 | **2011** | $71,250 |
| **2009** | $63,250 | **2012** | $74,750 |
| **2010** | $67,500 | **2013–2018** | $428,750 |

Expected benefits payments, net of participant contributions and expected Medicare Part D subsidies are as fol-lows (in actual dollars):

| | | | |
|---|---|---|---|
| **2008** | $481,000 | **2011** | $609,000 |
| **2009** | $516,500 | **2012** | $653,500 |
| **2010** | $560,000 | **2013 and on** | $3,955,250 |

The expected employer contribution in 2008 is $481,000.

## 7. Compositions of Net Assets

The compositions of the net assets of the university at the respective years ended on June 30 were as follows:

|  | 2007 | 2006 |
|---|---|---|
| Unrestricted net assets: | | |
| Undesignated – available for operating needs | $24,373 | $16,019 |
| Funds functioning as endowment and accumulated gains on permanent endowment whose income is unrestricted[a] | 79,079 | 77,874 |
| Investment in plant, net of long-term debt | 95,748 | 89,521 |
| | 199,200 | 183,414 |
| Temporarily restricted net assets: | | |
| Accumulated gains on permanent endowment whose income is restricted[a] | 39,211 | 36,911 |
| Amounts restricted by donors for specific purposes | 56,792 | 57,126 |
| Pledges receivable for specific purposes | 7,973 | 5,875 |
| | 103,976 | 99,912 |
| Permanently restricted net assets: | | |
| Permanent endowment and similar funds[a] | 224,223 | 124,173 |
| Pledges for permanent endowment[a] | 160,241 | 205,000 |
| | 384,464 | 329,173 |
| Total net assets | $687,640 | $612,499 |
| | | |
| [a] The sum of these items equals Total Endowment | $502,754 | $443,958 |

## 8. Commitments

The terms of certain limited partnership agreements require the university to periodically advance additional funding for private equity and real estate investments. At June 30, 2007, the university had commitments of approximately $15 million for which capital calls had not been exercised. Such commitments generally have fixed expiration dates or other termination clauses. The university maintains sufficient liquidity in its investment portfolio to cover such calls. Outstanding commitments for construction contracts amounted to approximately $10.6 million as of June 30, 2007.

# Bibliography

Abramson, Paul. "2006 College Construction Report." *College Planning and Management,* February 2006. *http://www.webcpm.com.*

American Institute of Certified Public Accountants. *Not-for-Profit Organizations—AICPA Audit and Accounting Guide.* (New York: AICPA, 2007).

APPA. *2004-05 Facilities Performance Indicators.* (Alexandria, Va.: APPA, 2006).

College and University Professional Association for Human Resources. "2006 Benefits Survey Report." *http://www.cupahr.org.*

——. "2005-06 National Faculty Salary Survey by Discipline and Rank in Four-Year Colleges and Universities." *http://www.cupahr.org/ surveys/salarysurvey2005-06.html.*

——. "2005-06 Administrative Compensation Survey." *http://www.cupahr.org/surveys/ salarysurvey2005-06.html.*

College Board. "Trends in College Pricing 2006." *http://www.collegeboard.com/trends.*

——. "Trends in Student Aid 2006." *http://www.collegeboard.com/trends.*

Committee of Sponsoring Organizations of the Treadway Commission. *Enterprise Risk Management—Integrated Framework.* (New York: The American Institute of Certified Public Accountants, 2004).

Commonfund Institute. "2006 Higher Education Price Index Report." *http://www. commonfund.org.*

Financial Accounting Standards Board. *Accounting for Certain Investments Held by Not-for-Profit Organizations.* Statement of Financial Accounting Standards (SFAS) no. 124, November 1995. Available online at *http://www.fasb.org/st/.*

——. *Accounting for Contributions Made and Contributions Received.* SFAS no. 116, June 1993. Available online at *http://www.fasb.org/st/.*

——. *Elements of Financial Statements.* Statement of Financial Accounting Concepts (SFAC) no. 6, December 1985. Available online at *http://www.fasb.org/st/.*

——. *Employers' Accounting for Postretirement Benefits Other Than Pensions.* SFAS no. 106, December 1990. Available online at *http://www.fasb.org/st/.*

——. *Financial Statements of Not-for-Profit Organizations.* SFAS no. 117, June 1993. Available online at *http://www.fasb.org/st/.*

——. *Objectives of Financial Reporting by Nonbusiness Organizations.* SFAC no. 4, December 1980. Available online at *http://www.fasb.org/st/.*

——. *Statement of Cash Flows.* SFAS no. 95, November 1987. Available online at *http://www.fasb.org/st/.*

Mattie, John A. and John H. McCarthy. "The Changing Role of the Audit Committee: Leading Practices for Colleges, Universities and Other Not-for-Profit Education Institutions." White paper, PricewaterhouseCoopers, 2004.

National Science Foundation. "Academic Research and Development Expenditures: Fiscal Year 2004." *http://www.nsf.gov/statistics/ nsf06323/.*

Office of the Attorney General, State of California, "Attorney General's Guide for Charities." *http://ag.ca.gov/charities/publications.php.*

Office of the New York State Attorney. "Internal Controls and Financial Accountability for Not-for-Profit Boards." *http://www.oag.state. ny.us/charities/charities.html.*

Strout, Erin. "College Endowments Post 'Respectable' Returns for 2005." *The Chronicle of Higher Education*, January 27, 2006.

———. "In the Money." *The Chronicle of Higher Education*, February 24, 2006.

Turner, Robert M. "An Examination of External Financial Reporting by Colleges and Universities." Ph.D. diss., Boston University, 1992.

Turner, Robert M., and Kenneth D. Williams. "Greater Accountability in Financial Reporting." In *Reinventing the University: Managing and Financing Institutions of Higher Education*, edited by Sandra L. Johnson and Sean C. Rush. New York: John Wiley and Sons, Inc., 1995.

U.S. Securities Exchange Commission. "Beginners' Guide to Financial Statements." *http://www.sec.gov/investor/pubs/ begfinstmtguide.htm.*

# Glossary

The following list of terms used throughout this book presents definitions in simplified terms. For more precise definitions, readers should refer to the FASB documents listed in the Bibliography, specifically SFAC No. 4, SFAC No. 6, and SFAS No. 116.

**Annual debt service.** Sum of interest expense and principal repayment. Used in ratio analysis, especially with operating and liquidity and cash flows ratios.

**Assets.** Items that an organization owns or controls and that have potential to be of service or future economic benefit. They are the results of past transactions. Examples include cash, investments, property, plant, and equipment.

**Contribution.** Voluntary, nonreciprocal gifts to a college or university. They can be either an asset, such as a monetary or in-kind donation, or a reduction of liability, such as the cancellation of an obligation. Formally referred to as "unconditional contribution."

**Donor-imposed condition.** Usually applied to pledges. Donor-required event or action that must occur before the transfer of an asset. If the institution fails to meet the condition(s), donors have the right to withdraw their promise to give.

**Donor-imposed restriction.** Usually applied to contributions. Donor-imposed limit of how the contribution may be used.

**Equity.** See "Net assets" definition.

**Expendable net assets.** Net assets that the institution can use for operating expenditures. Sum of unrestricted and temporarily restricted net assets minus net investment in plant. A special subset, "unrestricted expendable net assets," uses unrestricted net assets minus net investment in plant. Used in ratio analysis, especially with operating and financial strength ratios.

**Expenses.** Cash outflows caused by the production or delivery of an organization's goods and services. They can also be incurrences of liabilities. Examples include instruction, academic support, and administration.

**FASB.** Financial Accounting Standards Board. The organization in the private sector that establishes standards of financial accounting and reporting. Its counterpart is the Governmental Accounting Standards Board (GASB), which oversees government organizations, including public colleges and universities.

**Gains.** Increases in net assets caused by transactions outside the organization's operations. An example would be the settlement from a lawsuit. Gains may be classified as either operating or nonoperating.

**Generally Accepted Accounting Principles (GAAP).** The set of authoritative accounting and financial reporting standards developed by the FASB and other standard-setting bodies. GAAP is the minimum requirement for financial reporting.

**Higher Education Price Index (HEPI).** An inflation index designed by the Commonfund Institute specifically for higher education.

**Liabilities.** Sacrifices of economic benefit. They are future payments—or other obligations—of an organization resulting from a past transaction. Examples include accounts payable and long-term debt.

**Losses.** Decreases in net assets caused by transactions outside the organization's operations. An example would be damage to the campus caused by a natural disaster. Losses may be classified as either operating or nonoperating.

**Management Discussion and Analysis (MD&A).** Narrative explanation of the financial statements provided by management.

**Net assets.** The difference between an organization's assets and liabilities. For-profit businesses use the term "equity" for this same concept. Not-for-profit net assets are classified as permanently restricted, temporarily restricted, or unrestricted.

**Permanently restricted net assets.** Net assets bound by outside resource providers—donors, for example—who require the institution to retain their gifts indefinitely. True endowment funds are permanently restricted, as they are gifts made by donors who have specified that the principal (and sometimes a portion of its accumulated income) may not be spent.

**Promises to give.** A pledge, formally referred to as "unconditional promise to give." Colleges and universities should recognize pledges as revenue (equal to the net present value of the amounts expected to be received/realized) as long as verifiable documentation exists.

**Quasi endowment.** Board-designated funds to be invested as part of the institution's endowment.

**Revenues.** Inflows resulting from the provision of services or other activities related to an organization's operations. They increase an organization's assets. Examples include tuition revenue and investment income.

**Statement of activities.** Statement with aggregated information about the revenues, expenses, and other sources of funds of an institution. Overall, the statement of activities captures information about the operating activity of an institution, its investment management results, and its fundraising activities. Also called the "income statement."

**Statement of cash flows.** Statement with information about an institution's cash receipts and payments during a specific period. The cash flow statement should present separately cash flows from: (1) operating activities, (2) investing activities, and (3) financing activities.

**Statement of financial position.** Statement with a snapshot of an institution's financial condition at a particular point in time, generally the end of the fiscal year. The statement of financial position should display the following: (1) total assets, (2) total liabilities, (3) total net assets, and (4) totals for each of the three classes of net assets (unrestricted, temporarily restricted, and permanently restricted). Also called the "balance sheet."

**Temporarily restricted net assets.** Net assets whose donors (or resource providers) require the institution to use the gift for a specific purpose and after a period of time has transpired or after the institution fulfills a donor-stipulated action.

**Unrestricted net assets.** Net assets whose use the institution has full control of. All revenue and expense activity flows through unrestricted net assets.

# About the Authors

**John A. Mattie** is PricewaterhouseCooper's National Education and Nonprofit Practice Leader and currently serves as PwC's partner representative on the AICPA Government Audit Quality Control Center.

**John H. McCarthy** is the Senior Vice President for Administration and Finance at Northeastern University as well as a lecturer at Harvard University's Kennedy School of Government. He is also a retired partner of PricewaterhouseCoopers. He has published widely in the field.

**Robert M. Turner** is an Associate Professor of Accounting at Babson College. Professor Turner is widely published in the area of financial reporting of not-for-profit organizations.

**Sandra L. Johnson** is the former director of PricewaterhouseCoopers National Education Group, which coordinates the firm's services to colleges and universities.